Understanding Psychosis

Do psychotic disorders make sense? Are psychotic symptoms amenable to interpretation? *Understanding Psychosis: A Psychoanalytic Approach* takes the various pathways to psychotic illness outlined by psychoanalytic clinicians and scholars and integrates them into a model that allows a systematic assessment of relevant psychodynamic dimensions in the diagnosis of psychotic disorders, and which serves as a guide to psychotherapy with psychotically ill patients.

Joachim Küchenhoff reviews and integrates various psychoanalytic concepts and theories about psychosis into a multi-dimensional psychodynamic model that allows an assessment and understanding of the patient's subjective experience, objective psychological capabilities, and interpersonal resources. Küchenhoff helps the therapist to establish a basic attitude in working psychodynamically with patients and to understand the dynamics of the therapeutic relationship. *Understanding Psychosis* also addresses specific issues that can arise in work with clients experiencing psychosis, including understanding imminent crises or precursor states, elucidating semiotic qualities in seemingly negative symptoms, differentiating the psychotic and a non-psychotic part of the personality and providing a dynamic approach to the psychopharmacological treatment. Clinical vignettes and three detailed case reports are included in the book.

Understanding Psychosis will be an essential guide for psychiatrists, psychotherapists and psychoanalysts working with patients experiencing psychosis. It will also be of use to psychologists, and academics and students of psychotherapy, psychiatry and psychoanalysis for psychosis.

Joachim Küchenhoff, MD, is a psychoanalyst and member of the IPA and of the Swiss and German psychoanalytic societies. He is a specialist in psychiatry, psychotherapy and psychosomatic medicine, and is Professor of Psychiatry and Psychotherapy at the University of Basel, Switzerland. He has been working as the medical director of the department of adult psychiatry in Baselland, Switzerland, since 2007. He is editor-in-chief of the SANP (Swiss Archives of Neurology, Psychiatry and Psychotherapy), president of the supervisory board at IPU (International Psychoanalytic University) Berlin and member of many other advisory boards. He is author and editor of many previous publications.

Understanding Psychosis

A Psychoanalytic Approach

Joachim Küchenhoff

Translated by M. A. Luitgard Feiks and
Jürgen Muck

LONDON AND NEW YORK

First published in English 2018
by Routledge
2 Park Square, Milton Park, Abingdon, Oxon OX14 4RN

and by Routledge
711 Third Avenue, New York, NY 10017

Routledge is an imprint of the Taylor & Francis Group, an informa business

© 2018 Joachim Küchenhoff

The right of Joachim Küchenhoff to be identified as author of this work has been asserted by him in accordance with sections 77 and 78 of the Copyright, Designs and Patents Act 1988.

All rights reserved. No part of this book may be reprinted or reproduced or utilised in any form or by any electronic, mechanical, or other means, now known or hereafter invented, including photocopying and recording, or in any information storage or retrieval system, without permission in writing from the publishers.

This work is a translation of a work previously published in German as:
Joachim Küchenhoff: Psychose
© Psychosozial-Verlag, Gießen, 2012, www.psychosozial-verlag.de

Translated by M.A. Luitgard Feiks and Jürgen Muck

This translation was financially supported by Psychiatrie Baselland (Psychiatric Centre, Basel, Switzerland)

Trademark notice: Product or corporate names may be trademarks or registered trademarks, and are used only for identification and explanation without intent to infringe.

British Library Cataloguing in Publication Data
A catalogue record for this book is available from the British Library

Library of Congress Cataloging in Publication Data
Names: Küchenhoff, Joachim, author.
Title: Understanding psychosis : a psychoanalytic approach / Joachim Küchenhoff; translated by M.A. Luitgard Feiks and Jürgen Muck.
Other titles: Psychose. English
Description: Milton Park, Abingdon, Oxon; New York, NY : Routledge, 2018. | Includes bibliographical references.
Identifiers: LCCN 2018013567 (print) | LCCN 2018014233 (ebook) | ISBN 9781351025942 (Master e-book) | ISBN 9781138494664 (hbk) | ISBN 9781138494671 (pbk) | ISBN 9781351025942 (ebk)
Subjects: LCSH: Psychoses—Case studies. | Psychoanalysis—Case studies.
Classification: LCC RC512 (ebook) | LCC RC512.K8313 2018 (print) | DDC 616.89/17—dc23
LC record available at https://lccn.loc.gov/2018013567

ISBN: 978-1-138-49466-4 (hbk)
ISBN: 978-1-138-49467-1 (pbk)
ISBN: 978-1-351-02594-2 (ebk)

Typeset in Times New Roman
by Keystroke, Neville Lodge, Tettenhall, Wolverhampton

Printed and bound in Great Britain by
TJ International Ltd, Padstow, Cornwall

Contents

Preface   ix

1 Psychiatry, psychopathology and psychodynamics   **1**
Psychiatric classifications and the limitations of the
    psychiatric classification systems 1
Psychotic disorders in the ICD-10 5
Understanding psychopathology and the person of the
    psychotically ill patient 9
    An understanding- and meaning-oriented psychopathology
       and psychoanalysis 9
    The 'person' of the mentally ill 14
    Interpersonality and the 'recognition of the alien' 15

2 Psychoanalytic theories about psychosis   **21**
Psychosis as a defensive process and a remodelling of reality
    (according to Freud) 21
    Delusion as a projection of instinctual wishes 21
    Delusion as '*weltenaufgang*' 26
    Narcissism versus object relationship in psychosis 27
    Psychotic language and the return to the object 29
    The concrete thinking of the schizophrenic and the incapacity to
       symbolise 31
    The psychotic person's approach to reality 33
Pathological narcissism and relationship formation
    (after Freud) 35
    Psychogenesis and biogenesis are not incompatible
       opposites 35
    The psychotic and the body 37

The quality of psychotic object relationships 40
Autism and psychosis 44
Learning from experience in the psychotic process 47
Foreclosure and the symbolic order 50
The limits of language and the limits of thought 52
The vital importance of the recognition of difference –
 case example 54
The significance of destructiveness in psychosis 58
Experiential spaces and the development of
 representation 60
Pathological narcissism and the defence against
 triangulation 61
Psychotic solutions to basic conflicts of human
 relationships 63
Positivisation as a basic therapeutic attitude 65

**3 Conditions of psychotic experience: a psychodynamic
 factor model**   **69**
Preconditions 69
Formal structure of the factor model 70
Preconditions of psychotic disorders 71
Subjective experience 71
The objectifiable psychic capacities 78
The quality of object relationships 80
Conclusions from the factor model 83
The necessity of a multidimensional understanding of
 psychosis 83
The psychotherapist's basic attitude in working
 psychodynamically with psychotic patients 86
Relational dynamics and psychotic experience 87

4 Psychotherapeutic work with psychotic patients   **90**
The imminent loss of the reality-testing capacity 90
The compulsion to compensate for what the other is
 giving – a clinical example 92
*Psychotic residual conditions as a defence against
relationships 103*
The way of dealing with inner and outer walls – a literary
 case example 105

Contents vii

Psychotic and non-psychotic parts of the personality 112
    The covering up of the psychotic part of the personality
        through the non-psychotic part of the personality 113
    The covering up of the non-psychotic part of the personality
        through the psychotic part of the personality 115
Psychodynamics of the therapeutic relationship and the use of
    psychopharmacotropics within the treatment 118
    The application of medication viewed from the perspective
        of the therapeutic relationship 118
    Medication as a transference object 119
    Medication and newfound self-assertion and self-efficacy 121

**5   Psychotherapeutic engagement with psychotic patients:
concluding remarks   122**

References   125
Index   131

Preface

If – as actually occurred in 2011 – a 32-year-old man, after several years of meticulous planning and preparation, carries out a horrendous mass murder, and subsequently, although to at least some degree fully cognisant of his wrongdoings, claims it to be a courageous and heroic act of protest and resistance against the proliferation of socialism and Islam, and against contemporary society in general, then the question arises (and it is a pressing one) whether we are on the right track if we believe that we can judge this man's extreme and outrageous way of thinking and acting by the same psychological standards or criteria as are required when it comes to interacting with more or less ordinary people. And if, on top of it, the perpetrator claims membership to an order he calls the New Knights Templars and, as it were, to other forms of medieval brotherhoods or old-boy networks, thus insisting that he belongs to an organisation or movement that does not exist any longer, then the question forces itself upon us, if this man's thinking is not indeed to be viewed as highly delusional.

Seeking for a psychotic explanation or motivation for such a shocking and dreadful deed does actually serve one purpose and perhaps one purpose only: to pacify and calm people's destabilised minds in the face of such inconceivable horror. Just as the legal system provides for the mentally ill person the legal basis for the exemption of total or partial responsibility, it is also the case that for most people directly or indirectly affected by the mass killing, the diagnosis of a mental illness of the mass murderer would tend to have a mitigating effect. And so it is safe to say that the diagnosis of a psychotic illness at times may play an important regulating function that re-establishes the disrupted or lost order and the almost completely extinguished sense of hope and security, caused by the gravity of the offence committed, which lies so far beyond the scope of comprehension that one could justifiably say that the world has been turned upside down. Hence, it appears to be this imagination of it being 'simply and exclusively' due to the murderous impulses of one single person's severely disturbed and ill mind capable of a deed which unhinged the world that will finally help people to regain their former sense of serenity and peace of mind.

If a poet like Friedrich Hölderlin, who proves to be not only a revolutionary and radical theoretical thinker, but who over and above that in his use of the German language pushes beyond the traditional boundaries of expression, at a certain point in his life loses his ability to cope with day-to-day life and, as a corollary of that, has to be provided with medical treatment, special care and assistance, because his emotional and mental torment at a certain point in time became so excessive and overwhelming that he was diagnosed as psychotic, then this kind of diagnosis automatically impeaches the poet's credibility and casts doubt on his poetic skills. His entire work, his ideas and his language performance with its specific linguistic expressiveness are now being put under scrutiny and analysed, exclusively with a view to detect and discover the first and clandestine signs of a severe oncoming mental illness. The admirers of the poet consider this psychiatric assessment simply as a disgrace, as if this casts a slur on the poet's sublime spirit; they come up with all sorts of explanations and ideas in order to negate and ignore his personal suffering and instead prefer to view his idiosyncrasies as a wilful performance or even an act of political wisdom. And then there are those who, on the other hand, never were favourably inclined towards the poet and his work, and on whom his poems had always exerted a more or less disturbing and unsettling effect, and who now with this psychiatric diagnosis have a hit on their hands, which finally allows them to debunk his ideas and beliefs and to expose the greatness of his poetic work as a myth, and even to discount and dismiss it as the ramblings of a deeply disturbed and troubled mind (Gonther and Schlimme 2011).

These two examples mentioned above make us aware of the serious consequences and different reactions the diagnosis of a psychotic disorder may provoke: apart from the medical factors it brings to the fore various other factors as well. Obviously, there is first of all the interpersonal factor to be considered, which brings to mind the important issue of appreciation and respect towards the person concerned. Time and again we can see it happening that the diagnosis of a psychotic illness is doing considerable harm to the reputation of a person, but, in a certain way, the reverse situation is possible too. In the case of the mass murderer, for instance, the diagnosis of a psychotic disorder rescues the reputation of the culprit, at least to a certain extent; whereas in the case of the poet such a diagnosis may be capable of undermining and even ruining the poet's previously good reputation. But besides that, there is also the social factor to be kept in mind which, among other things, concerns the person's ability to carry legal and criminal responsibility. But incidentally, it also concerns issues of social acceptance and respect or social ostracism. In any case, the diagnosis of a mental illness or psychotic disorder may lead to the individual being discriminated and marginalised and thus being not taken seriously any more. Such a diagnosis can exert tremendous power; and this is actually one of the ways in which power in society is exercised.

The way in which psychotically ill individuals are both cared for and treated tells us a great deal about how tolerant or intolerant a society is towards abnormalities, oddities and eccentricities, that is, towards the unfamiliar in general. There is still a widespread stigma attached to a psychiatric diagnosis, but even more so to a diagnosis of a psychotic disorder. The majority of psychiatric hospitals still carry names, which are no longer the official ones but are, nevertheless, still used in the common parlance, and which evidently bear testimony to the misery of the mentally ill patients cared for and treated in those institutions in a time long since gone: the 'Friedmatt' in Basle, the 'Hasenbühl' in Liestal, the 'Wiesloch' for the psychiatric clinic in Wiesloch, the 'Schlangengrube' in Vienna, and so on. Clearly, the issue of psychotic disorders can no longer be discussed without taking account of the relation between 'madness and civilisation', to use the phrase of Foucault (1984).

Both of the above-mentioned examples also reflect the potential adverse effects on people's minds in case of being confronted with individuals diagnosed as psychotic: the majority of the people is still enticed by the diagnosis of a psychotic disorder to view it as absolutely contradictory and antagonistic to certain human faculties or capacities, such as the responsibility for one's own actions or, for instance, the poetic and linguistic competence. Psychotic symptoms are therefore bound to be considered as occupying the whole of the person. And accordingly one habitually says: 'the patient *is* psychotic', rather than saying: 'the patient *has* a psychotic illness'. One important reason for this lies in the subject itself – in other words, there is also a '*fundamentum in re*', which is likely to be responsible for that in the past psychotic disturbances were commonly referred to as 'diseases of the mind' and in everyday language those patients were simply called mad (in German: *ver-rückt*, which literally means *dis-placed*). Still today we refer to such individuals as having lost their mind, or as being out of their mind. After all, the choice of words, in a certain sense at least, hits the point and thus is not that far away from the truth. But regardless of how we would prefer to call it, in every case the individual's way of perceiving and experiencing himself or herself and the world has gone out of shape or gotten out of place, or put differently, his sense of reality is distorted or '*ver-rückt*'. The psychotic patient is now deprived of his usual understanding of self and the surrounding world, because the previously acquired and self-evident faculties of the mind are not any longer automatically and reliably at his disposal.

Psychotic disorders are the manifestations of a profound change in a person's mode of thinking, perceiving, feeling and acting, as a corollary of which the individual almost invariably is being deprived of his self-reflective capacities, which otherwise would allow him to assume a self-critical stance and self-distanced perspective from which to recognise and acknowledge – or else foreclose – the now altered mode of thinking and experiencing. In some cases the lack of insight into the psychotic illness even renders impossible or impracticable any form of therapy. It is first and foremost this lack of insight that impedes the patient's relation to his inner and outer world, and which puts considerable strain on the relationship to the therapists, but likewise on that to the immediate family and close relatives. And this is also the reason why in certain severe cases enforced treatment may be advisable. However, if that is the case, the patient who anyhow feels already intensely persecuted, disempowered and dispossessed of everything he ever had, now all the more feels caught up and trapped in a network of evil conspiracies and devious power games.

xii Preface

Psychotic symptoms are usually the outcome of a profound and radical change in a person's thinking and feeling in the wake of overwhelming mental strain, and that's why they are always experienced as extremely taxing and stressful no matter what caused them originally. The symptoms can take on a variety of forms. And what's more, psychotic experiences cannot easily be 'forgotten', irrespective of the factors that induced or provoked them, since they are always a very carving experience for the person concerned. An alcoholic withdrawal delirium, for instance, produces specific hallucinations. Most of the biological processes involved are well known today and can be described and explained in detail. All the same, these hallucinations feel so unwaveringly real that the experience remains firmly etched into the individual's memory. Even if it is more than likely that the alcohol respectively the withdrawal of it, is accountable for having unleashed the psychotic episode or crisis, it is, nevertheless, true that the hallucinations experienced by the individual cannot be argued away. In regard to the individual's sense of reality any psychotic episode represents a severe rupture and that's why it is such a deeply upsetting and alarming experience which stays in the individual's mind and subverts his natural sense of 'everyday self-evidentiality' (Blankenburg 1971).

So, the discussion in this book deals with illnesses that have without exception a profoundly unsettling effect on the patient's subjective experience of everyday life, and which jeopardise his conception of and relationship to himself and the world. But they also considerably interfere with the patient's social life. This situation is made even worse by the fact that it is not at all easy to treat such illnesses, particularly if, on the part of the patient, any insight into his illness ('compliance') including the motivation for treatment are lacking.

Now, the question arises: If the patient has to a certain degree lost his sense of reality, in other words, if it has been displaced ('*ver-rückt*'), does this necessarily imply that the psychotic experiencing is therefore meaningless? Or, is there a real possibility to understand and find symbolic meanings in the psychotic patient's existence? And if so, how can we practically achieve this? To even ask this question has been far from being self-evident in the course of the history of psychiatry to this day. A series of complex steps are required prior to asking this question.

The first step means to no longer consider merely the form of psychotic production but, in addition to that, ask or search for its contents as well, in order to then create a link between these two seemingly opposing aspects. To ask for the meaning of psychotic experience implies to not only derive some kind of diagnosis from the examination of the patient's distorted or dis-placed form of experiencing but instead to carefully listen to what the psychotically ill patient has to say; in other words, to take seriously what the patient has to say and to allow to be reached and emotionally touched by it.

By this we have already addressed what is involved in the second step. Once we have replaced the medical-diagnostic, objectifying approach by an interactional or intersubjective one, we come to realise that already the assessment of a psychopathological condition has to basically arise from a social encounter or interaction between two individuals. Johann Glatzel (1978) for his part has described the psychopathological diagnostics as representing the failure or else the success of a 'consensual situation definition'. But this interactional aspect consists not only of agreement processes. Unlike in the case of a merely medical disorder the diagnostic findings in the case of the mentally ill patient are also the result of a sometimes conflictual negotiation and mediation: in any case, those diagnostic findings have been constituted and constructed in the attempt to establish contact with the symbolic meanings of the psychotic patient's existence. Thus it appears that the diagnostician's attitude towards the mentally ill or psychotic patient plays a major role, since it essentially determines what he sees and what he hears. And this situation of interpersonal encounter contains the essence of the active ingredient needed not only for the psychotherapeutic situation, but already prior to that for the diagnostic situation.

Finally, with the third step we are going to extend the intersubjective perspective on the understanding of the psychotic symptoms even further: the clinician has to try to intuitively understand what the mentally ill individual has to say to the other and, furthermore, he has to figure out whom this other represents in the mind (i.e. in the inner relational world of the patient). What needs to be considered while establishing rapport with the patient is the quality of his relational experiences during his entire life-span in order to comprehend and better understand why the patient in the actual encounter of the assessment situation conducts himself exactly in the way he does, and not otherwise, since the inner voice of the patient is persistent until it has secured a hearing. And so the diagnostic findings are viewed as a response: the symptom responds to the other, namely the one who once injured and failed the patient and who violated his boundaries by being too intrusive – in whatever form.

To engage in such a way with the mentally ill (*Der Geisteskranke als Mitmensch* – Benedetti 1983) is a major challenge to any clinician or therapist. The current book assembles the various psychoanalytic concepts which altogether have proved to be a most valuable contribution in order to gain a more profound and comprehensive understanding of psychosis, which is indispensable to take seriously and do justice to the mentally ill individual. It is, however, not the principal concern of this book to provide an informative and comprehensive historical account but rather I am going to endeavour to bring together two relevant aspects: one important aspect I'm going to elaborate on in this book concerns the therapist's attitude required when encountering and trying to establish emotional rapport with the psychotic patient; and secondly, a specific factor model will provide an overview over the vast range of therapeutic diagnostic approaches.

In the discussion of the current book I shall confine myself to dealing with the issues of delusional psychotic and schizophrenic disorders. Excluded from my discussion are major depressive disorders with prominent psychotic features. Because of their enormous complexity these disorders and the specific dynamics involved deserve to be discussed and analysed independently.

I would like to end this introduction with the wish to express my sincere gratitude towards all co-workers supporting the book to be published in English. It is a great honour for me that it comes out at Routledge. I am especially indebted to the editorial assistant, Elliott Morzia, and the copy-editor, Hamish Ironside, who took care of the manuscript and accompanied the editing process in a very attentive and diligent manner. I am profoundly grateful to the translators Luitgard Feiks and Jürgen Muck, who worked on the manuscript with a maximum of sensitivity and great prudence and care to ensure the successful publication of the book. Last but not least I want to thank Hans-Jürgen Wirth, the editor of the Psychosozial-Verlag in Germany, without whose support this book in its original German version would not have been possible, and whose encouragement gave me the confidence and courage to have it translated and thus accessible to the English-speaking reader.

Chapter 1

Psychiatry, psychopathology and psychodynamics

Psychiatric classifications and the limitations of the psychiatric classification systems

As a generic concept the term 'psychosis' has almost completely disappeared from the psychiatric classification systems by now. Although we still can find the term 'psychotic' in the ICD-10 (WHO 2016) as well as in the DSM-5 (APA 2013), it is no longer applied in order to describe a wider spectrum of mental suffering. Although it is to be expected that the ICD-11 will provide in the near future a more differentiated assessment of the acute psychotic disorders, we can assume that there will be no major change or significant shift in the fundamental approach. The use of the term 'psychosis' as a generic concept was historically justified, as it covered a spectrum of mental disorders not to be subsumed under the opposite generic term of 'neurosis', a concept, which is also practically no longer used in psychiatric diagnosis today.

In the past neurosis was defined as a functional mental disorder involving specific symptoms that do not affect and impair the individual's whole personality, since apart from the neurotic parts of the personality the more healthy parts of the personality continue to persist. It was once the accepted view that neurosis was largely the human psyche's response to excessive and unresolved mental strain and stress often originating in early childhood.

Psychosis, by contrast, was considered as a condition of the mind which involved a loss of contact with reality and difficulties with social interaction, and that's why it was viewed as affecting the whole person. But as it is frequently the case, the nomenclature refers to the aetiology and pathogenesis of the disease. Neurosis was considered as being the product of an unfavourable developmental history marked by predominantly adverse and stressful learning experiences; or else the product of a psychic conflict that had to be denied and repressed, so that the conflict was permanently banned from consciousness only to then manifesting itself indirectly in the form of a symptom. Accordingly the hypothesis was made that while psychoses are always the result of somatic illness and are therefore a disease process, neuroses have psychological biographical causes and are therefore a development on a continuum with health. The dichotomy of process and

2 Psychiatry, psychopathology, psychodynamics

development was followed by a dichotomisation of methods, natural causal explanations of psychoses, on the one hand, and psychological comprehension of neuroses on the other. So, following this line of argumentation, neuroses were basically thought of as psychogenic diseases, whereas psychoses were considered as being either organically caused ('exogenous psychosis') or else as being the result of more or less unknown biological processes ('endogenous psychosis'). But that there might be something in between these two positions, that is, the possibility of a so-called psychogenic psychosis, or to put it differently, that psychotic suffering could also arise from psychic conflict, this has been the subject of a controversial debate for a very long time. Take, for instance, hysterical psychosis, which belongs to this category and which essentially corresponds to what Freud described as a 'psychosis marked by a state of over-dramatisation': the hysterical mechanism escalates and thus finally develops a momentum of its own, so that in the end the individual is completely caught up and trapped in his own theatrical enactments and hysterical dramatisations.

Looking back, it stands out even more noticeably that this very strong dichotomising tendency, reflected in the choice of terminology mentioned above, whereby descriptive and aetiologically relevant theories and concepts are unduly confused and mixed-up, did not in any way contribute to the reduction of the existing prejudices. And so it is hardly surprising that something had to be done about this and that eventually it was decided that the clinical diagnostics had to be radically renewed. In the ICD-10 the concept of illness or disease was dropped and eliminated, and instead the concept 'disorder' was introduced with the following explanation: 'The term "disorder" is used throughout the classification, so as to avoid even greater problems inherent in the use of terms such as "disease" and "illness"' (WHO 2016).

And thus we can see, the concept 'disorder' first of all bears significance in that it seems to serve a 'negative' function, namely: the function to 'negate' the other existing concepts. By choosing an ultimately empty and more or less meaningless concept it was intended to dismiss the narrowing and one-sided nosological thinking where diseases are often prematurely classified by their cause or aetiology, or one could say, by the mechanisms by which the disease is caused or by its symptoms. And so the hope was that the use of the concept 'disorder' would be an incentive to call into question received ideas and old and long-established thought patterns and to thus expand our field of vision. Although one had to soon admit to the shortcomings and problems the introduction of such a non-specific concept as 'disorder' involved, it was nevertheless considered as valuable and as having primarily the function of escaping the influence of the dominant nosographical grid with its detrimental effect that frequently only those symptoms are investigated that are supposed to have a diagnostic value, a fact that consequently excludes the scrutiny of the manifold manifestations of what is really there in the patients' experience, which is, after all, the essential prerequisite to understanding the inner and outer worlds our patients live in. And thus the concept 'disorder' was basically used 'to imply the existence of a clinically recognizable set of symptoms or behaviour associated in most cases with distress and with interference with personal functions' (WHO 2016).

We can thus retain that the term 'disorder' was deliberately chosen in order to make available to psychiatry and psychopathology a neutral nosological concept. It should be said, though, that the concept did not achieve this aim, because, subtly and involuntarily, disorders would once again be viewed as diseases. As ever the language being used is telling. Is it not a sign of the return of the repressed if one, all good intentions notwithstanding, continues to use a term like 'co-morbidity' whenever the presence of one or more additional disorders is co-occurring with a primary disorder? As is well known, *morbus* designates illness or disease. Certainly, the use of the term 'co-morbidity' opposes the basic idea of neutrality and, by the same token, refutes the negation of the idea of disease that the concept 'disorder' pretends to pursue.

The second main objective was to create a method of diagnostic classification, which is free of theory and thus foregoes the prejudices of aetiological concepts. The goal was to replace any theory-led or theory-driven prejudices by a rigorous and precise description of the specific phenomena. This, of course, implied to adopt a phenomenological position in the attempt to abstract from, that is, leave aside all of the currently existing theoretical approaches including their theoretical and conceptual prejudices with the explicit aim to go back to the phenomena *per se*, each of which can (and probably has to) be interpreted differently. The inventories of the classification systems had set themselves the task of being strictly and exclusively descriptive: according to certain predefined criteria the various behavioural patterns and modes of experience are broken down into a great number of psychiatric diagnoses. This in turn results in a broad array of diagnoses that in its sheer diversity and complexity bears the risk of becoming so complex and thus confusing that in the end the clinician may be left without a clue.

In view of this situation the question has to be asked: Is a discipline – a science – that relies upon a 'theory-free' *modus operandi* at all possible? It should however, and I shall say this from the start, be noted that such a claim would contradict the principles of any hermeneutics. And this is actually also in line with Hans-Georg Gadamer's famous critique of the 'prejudice against prejudices', in which pre-conceptions are seen not only as obstacles but as inevitable and enabling compo-nents of any process of knowing (Gadamer 1960). The philosopher even claimed that prejudices are the ground on which we can experience at all; and furthermore he stated that it is a fact that one's own worldview does not develop '*ab ovo*', instead we construct reality according to the various traditions incorporated into our languages and cultures.

Now, the further question would be then: What exactly is the *modus operandi* of diagnostic classification? What one can definitely say about this is that the method of rigorously describing the diagnostic findings boils down to a method which dispenses with all contextual thinking, and which instead collects and lists meticulously and in a non-hierarchical order the entirety of the pathological syn-dromes observed without looking at them in a wider perspective or without putting

4 Psychiatry, psychopathology, psychodynamics

them in context to each other. This diagnostic classification method that pretends that it can operate without any pre-suppositions and without any theoretical prejudices, depends solely on its own algorithms for the criteriology of every single diagnosis, thereby disregarding aspects of subjective experience and biography, a method which is predicated on – and this already has to be considered a theoretical basic position – what has become known as an elemental psychology. The idea behind this was to empower psychiatry with a valid and reliable method, which enables the psychiatrist to assess and determine the pathological mental states in their patients. To this purpose, Karl Jaspers in his *Allgemeine Psychopathologie* [*General Psychopathology*] (1913) created an approach where he broke up the mental state of his patients in single elements or isolated entities to bring order into the chaos of abnormal psychic phenomena by way of rigorous description, definition and classification. The resulting descriptive phenomenology with its analysis of isolated mental entities has served as the basis for psychopathology in the field of psychiatry until today, one hundred years later.

In the German-speaking countries the system of the AMDP (Broome et al. 2017) has become widely accepted. It particularly helps the young psychiatrist in his continuous process of education to learn to distinguish between different types of pathological conditions, when he is faced, for instance, with the following questions: Is it a hallucination? Is it a thought disorder? Is there a cohesive sense of self or not? Do the affects appear mood-congruent or mood-incongruent? Etcetera, etcetera . . . To identify all these specific entities or isolated mental features may then provide the ground for a diagnosis. Let's, for example, consider the issue of thought disorders: 'flight of ideas' is always an indication of a manic condition; schizophrenic thinking, by contrast, appears incoherent and absent-minded or scatter-brained. Although no single mental feature allows one to establish a diagnosis, it nevertheless, may prove an essential element in the process of eventually reaching a valid and reliable diagnosis (cf. Scharfetter 2002). But what is falling irrevocably by the wayside with this phenomenological approach is the psychology of meaningful connections. Let's just for a moment consider such an example as a thought disorder, where the view at the wider perspective might be worth taking and one might thus ask the following questions: Are there particular conversational situations with specific persons, or perhaps particular issues that, whenever addressed, could be considered as triggering the symptoms of the thought-disorder?

Such a mechanical, simplistic and elementary application of a merely criteriological approach implies that diagnostic entities are empirically derived on descriptive 'primary' sources of data, which are, in effect, the clinician's account of psychological constructs. And these constructs or definitions seem entirely based on an 'operationalisation' of the psychiatric diagnostic process which is in line with particular algorithms. While the introduction of operationalised diagnosis in psychiatry was once deemed a useful accomplishment, it has subsequently brought to light evidences of its major short-comings. Mind, for instance, that the clinician's constructs, or definitions, as it were, are unavoidably reductive and conventional, since in the clinician's attempt to verbally pin down his observation and find a suitable definition for it, he has necessarily to conform with the linguistic usage, etc. The clinical gaze looking for specific criteria necessarily selects from the great variety of clinical data and thus blanks out and excludes other possible data contents and therefore inevitably ignores possible relevant contexts. And do not forget that the selection of the criteria as such will always depend on some sort of interpretation.

The claim of an atheoretical or theory-free approach is detrimental, since it bears the fundamental risk of, firstly, promising something that, as a matter of principle, cannot be fulfilled, and since it, secondly, disregards certain tacit and implicit presuppositions that – all the same and all the more – exert a decisive influence on the clinical approach. Following this line of argumentation it has to be stated that it is an epistemological requirement to consider the applied criteria as being prejudices, as theoretical presuppositions. To not obscure this fact, but rather bring it to light may help us to become aware of the underlying 'biases' or 'theoretical filters' and scrutinise them as best as we can. But this is far from common practice today. Unfortunately, the claim for a theory-free diagnostics still hasn't been laid to rest and thus continues to distract from the fact that any discipline inevitably relies on theoretical presuppositions which, of course, we must never cease to critically scrutinise and reflect upon.

One should certainly not obscure the fact that the diagnostic classification systems create new conventions and new preconceptions with the unfortunate result that they may then exclude the scrutiny of the manifold clinical manifestations of what is really there in the patient's experience. These classification systems create the language for the many dialects and jargons spoken by the clinicians in the field of mental health, who then are liable to (mis-)take this common language for the reality (i.e. for the knowledge of the phenomena of experience they pretend to grasp). Although they seem to be promising and facilitating in several ways, these classification systems, at the same time, impede other valuable and alternative ways of understanding and looking at things. Against this background we strongly advocate that an epistemological discourse analysis should stand at the beginning of any serious debate. Such an epistemological analysis may open our horizon for alternative perspectives left out and neglected in the diagnostic classification systems of the DSM and ICD. And one of these alternative perspectives most certainly is the psychoanalytic approach.

Psychotic disorders in the ICD-10

Whatever justified criticism may have been levelled at them, it is not possible to flinch from taking notice of the diagnostic classification systems, which nevertheless form a uniform standard for the common technical terminology in psychiatry. The current book mainly focusses upon the psychodynamics of psychosis, and not upon the descriptive diagnostics. In spite of that, it may be of some relevance to become, to a certain extent at least, familiar with some of the clinical

6 Psychiatry, psychopathology, psychodynamics

pictures linked to the concept of 'psychosis'. What follows therefore is a brief overview of the psychotic disorders as described in the ICD-10.

First, reference is made to the different types of schizophrenia and the schizotypal and delusional disorders, which are listed under F 20 to F 29.

Paranoid schizophrenia (F 20.0) is dominated by relatively stable, often paranoid delusions, usually accompanied by hallucinations, particularly of the auditory variety and perceptual disturbances.

Hebephrenic schizophrenia (F 20.1) is a form of schizophrenia that is normally only diagnosed in adolescents and young adults, and in which affective changes are prominent, delusions and hallucinations fleeting and fragmentary, behaviour irresponsible and unpredictable, and mannerisms common. The mood is shallow and inappropriate, thought is disorganised, and speech is incoherent. There is a tendency to social isolation.

Catatonic schizophrenia (F 20.2) is dominated by prominent psychomotor disturbances that may alternate between extremes such as hyperkinesis and stupor, or automatic obedience and negativism.

In the ICD-10 undifferentiated schizophrenia (F 20.3) is characterised by psychotic conditions meeting the general diagnostic criteria, but not conforming to any of the subtypes (F 20.0–20.2).

Post-schizophrenic depression (F 20.4) – here only briefly referred to – is followed by residual schizophrenia (F 20.5). It is described as a chronic stage in the development of a schizophrenic illness in which there has been a clear progression from an early stage to a later stage characterised by long-term though not necessarily irreversible, 'negative' symptoms, such as psychomotor slowing; underactivity; blunting of affect; passivity and lack of initiative; poverty of quantity or content of speech; poor nonverbal communication by facial expression, eye contact, voice modulation and posture; poor self-care and social performance.

Simple schizophrenia (F 20.6) is described as a disorder in which there is an insidious but progressive development of oddities of conduct, inability to meet the demands of society, and decline in total performance. The characteristic negative features of residual schizophrenia (e.g. blunting of affect and loss of volition) develop without being preceded by any overt psychotic symptoms (anxiety, delusion, hallucinations etc.).

F 20.8 refers to other forms of schizophrenia. F 20.9 refers to schizophrenia, unspecified. Schizotypal disorders (F 21) are characterised by eccentric behaviour and anomalies of thinking, and affect which resemble those seen in schizophrenia, though no definite and characteristic schizophrenic anomalies occur at any stage. In the DSM-5 these disorders are attributed to the group of personality disorders.

If we are concerned with psychotic disorders, we must not forget to also pay special attention to the purely delusional modes of experience, where other characteristic features of schizophrenic disorders are not present, and only delusion is prominent. Delusion is, according to Gruhle (1953), a 'delusion of reference'. This means that the deluded subject relates a specific external event exclusively to himself, whereby the deluded subject often feels watched, followed or controlled by it. For instance, the subject may be convinced that the TV news presenter sends an unmistakeably accusatory message to him.

Under F 22 persistent delusional disorders are described as a variety of disorders in which long-standing delusions constitute the only, or the most conspicuous, clinical characteristic and which cannot be classified as organic, schizophrenic or affective.

Delusional disorder (F 22.0) is a disorder characterised by the development either of a single delusion or of a set of related delusions that are usually persistent and sometimes lifelong. The content of the delusion or delusions is very variable. Clear and persistent auditory hallucinations (voices), schizophrenic symptoms such as delusions of control and marked blunting of affect, and definite evidence of brain disease are all incompatible with this diagnosis. However, the presence of occasional or transitory auditory hallucinations, particularly in elderly patients, does not rule out this diagnosis, provided that they are not typically schizophrenic and form only a small part of the overall clinical picture.

Other persistent delusional disorders (F 22.8) are described as disorders in which delusion or delusions are accompanied by schizophrenic symptoms that do not justify a diagnosis of schizophrenia.

The category F 23, acute and transient psychotic disorders is a heterogeneous group of disorders characterised by the acute onset of psychotic symptoms such as delusions, hallucinations, and perceptual disturbances, and by the severe disruption of ordinary behaviour. Acute onset is defined as crescendo development of a clearly abnormal clinical picture in about two weeks or less. For these disorders there is no evidence of organic or toxic causation. Perplexity and puzzlement are often present but disorientations for time, place and person is not persistent or severe enough to justify a diagnosis of organically caused delirium. Complete recovery usually occurs within a few months, often within a few weeks or even days. The disorder may or may not be associated with acute stress, defined as usually stressful events preceding the onset by one to two weeks.

This group includes the acute polymorphic psychotic disorder without symptoms of schizophrenia (F 23.0), which describes an acute, psychotic disorder in which hallucinations, delusions or perceptual disturbances are obvious but markedly variable, changing from day to day or even from hour to hour. Emotional turmoil with intense transient feelings of happiness or ecstasy, or anxiety and irritability, is also frequently present. The polymorphism and instability are characteristic for the overall clinical picture and the psychotic features do not justify a diagnosis of schizophrenia. Acute polymorphic disorder with symptoms of schizophrenia (F 23.1) is an acute disorder in which the polymorphic and unstable clinical picture is present; despite this instability, however, some symptoms typical of schizophrenia are also in evidence for the majority of the time.

Acute schizophrenia-like psychotic disorder (F 23.2) is an acute psychotic disorder in which the psychotic symptoms are comparatively stable and justify a diagnosis of schizophrenia, but have lasted for less than about a month. Under F 23.3 acute delusional psychotic disorders are described as acute psychotic disorders in which comparatively stable delusions or hallucinations are the main clinical features, but do not justify a diagnosis of schizophrenia.

For the depressive disorders normally a profound change in affect and mood is characteristic. In the ICD-10 severe depressive episodes with psychotic symptoms are described in a separate category. The severe depressive episode with psychotic symptoms (F 32.3) is an episode of depression with the presence of hallucinations, delusions, psychomotor retardation, or stupor so severe that ordinary social activities are impossible; there may be a danger to life from suicide, dehydration, or starvation. The hallucinations and delusions may or may not be mood-congruent. The same applies to mania, where delusions and hallucinations may be present, too. In mania with psychotic symptoms (F 30.2) delusions (usually grandiose) or hallucinations (usually of voices speaking directly to the patient) are present.

Psychotic episodes may be induced by psychoactive substances. The most common of these substances are the hallucinogenic drugs. The ICD-10 subsumes the different psychoactive substances that may induce mental and behavioural disorders under F 10–19.

Finally, psychotic disorders may result from physical disease and brain dysfunction. This category includes miscellaneous conditions causally related to brain disorder due to primary cerebral disease, to systemic disease affecting the brain secondarily, to exogenous toxic substances or hormones, to endocrine disorders, or to other somatic illnesses (F 06). Psychotic states associated with delirium are listed separately under F 05. Organic hallucinosis (F 06.0) is a disorder of persistent or recurrent hallucinations, usually visual or auditory that occur in clear consciousness and may or may not be recognised by the subject as such. Delusional elaboration of the hallucinations may occur, but delusions do not dominate the clinical picture; insight may be preserved. F 06.1 describes the organic catatonic disorder. F 06.2 describes the organic delusional (schizophrenia-like) disorder.

There is, as the above descriptions have clearly shown, a wide spectrum of subtle forms of experience and expressions or reactions, which are classified as 'psychotic'. So the fact remains that we cannot only speak in general terms of 'psychosis', and that it is normally not the result of one *single* cause. Suffice it to say here, classification may, at best, be viewed as a starting point in that it offers the clinician or therapist certain sophisticated descriptive and conceptual tools for precisely observing and monitoring what can be directly perceived through the senses in regard to the patient's self-experience. But classification is certainly unsuitable to overcome the gap between the two positions of that of the therapist and that of the patient viewed as a unique human being with his/her particular personality, disposition and biography. All those therapists, whose major concern it is to establish a personal rapport with the patient in order to capture something of the reality and truth of the patient's self-experience and thus help him/her to overcome the psychotic crisis, can only feel marooned and let down by this exclusively descriptive approach offered by the classification systems.

Understanding psychopathology and the person of the psychotically ill patient

An understanding- and meaning-oriented psychopathology and psychoanalysis

A purely descriptive psychopathology does not in any substantial way contribute to the understanding of the real experience of the mentally ill person: for example, to describe the experiential phenomena of a depression does not explain the genesis and development of the depressive condition. Describing, for instance, a panic attack as episodic paroxysmal anxiety (i.e. as a seemingly unmotivated anxiety) does not provide any causal explanation of it, nor even suggest that it may, at least partly, be due to some kind of biochemical imbalance. Although the two standardised diagnostic manuals ICD and DSM have deliberately set themselves the task of avoiding the question of cause and effect regarding psychotic disorders, they at the same time – mindfully or unmindfully – have accepted the fact that this implies the relinquishment of the deeper understanding of these conditions. Yet without such an understanding people suffering from mental illness cannot be helped as their situation requires.

The internationally recognised psychotherapy researcher David Orlinsky (2003) has argued that the genesis of a disease can only be illuminated through the discovery and careful reconstruction of the pathogenic process without taking into consideration the symptoms produced by this process. Otherwise one may fall prey to some kind of circular reasoning (cf. Küchenhoff 2003). What's meant by this might best be elucidated with the help of examples. The first example refers to Karl Jaspers (1913), who postulated that psychosis is organically caused. He argued that it is always the result of somatic illness and therefore to be considered a disease process; and hence Jasper's claim of a purely endogenous psychosis that can only be explained but not psychologically comprehended. But the assumption of such an organically caused disease process represents a mere act of positing. On the basis of the clinical picture and the progression of the illness it is simply concluded, or rather, short-circuited, that psychosis is not comprehensible but only explainable. Imagine for instance: I listen to what the psychotic person has to say, and I consider it as nonsense, and I further assume that this nonsense is caused by a neurobiological malfunction, which again justifies me not paying any further heed to what the patient is saying, with the inevitable result of myself from now on hearing the patient just talking nonsense.

A second example: today the movement operations between 'surface' and 'deep' layers (i.e. between phenomena and deep structure processes) are short-circuited in another way. If, for example, in the event of a disorder of cortisol production, it is concluded that the patient must be suffering from depression irrespective of the patient's manifesting depressive symptoms or not, this clearly is a case of short circuit as well. This time it is short-circuited from the concrete biological processes to the phenomenon, and not, the other way around, from the phenomenon to the underlying process. What is lacking in both examples is

10 Psychiatry, psychopathology, psychodynamics

the independent description of, and the mediation between, the 'symptom' and the 'process' level.

After all it must be stated that pathogenic processes may be attributed to biological or to psychological causes, or else to both coincidently. Besides, one should always keep in mind that the interrelations between the symptoms and the genesis of the disease are extremely complex. In the current discussion I am primarily focussing on the psychological 'underpinnings' of the mental disorders. What's in this context of particular relevance is the psychoanalytic or psychodynamic diagnostics. Its main objective is to expand or even replace the descriptive classification by a diagnostics that is based upon the description of the characteristic features of a *potential* psychological process underlying the disorder. The description of longstanding and pathogenic psychic conflicts, the determination of the degree of the person's integration capacities, the analysis of dysfunctional relational patterns (OPD Task Force 2009), all these are significant components that serve the one function, namely to find out the various psychological patterns, which have a decisive influence upon the patient's mode of experiencing and feeling, and which can be considered as the missing link between the two opposite poles of symptom, on the one hand, and biological process on the other. The psychodynamic approach has acceded to the heritance of a psychopathology which saw itself to be not merely and exclusively a descriptive psychopathology (see especially Küchenhoff 2006a).

For quite a long period of time psychopathology saw itself as a 'basic science' in the field of psychiatry. With the focus upon the exploration of the subjective experiences of people with mental illnesses psychiatric research acknowledged the coexistence of a number of different methods of approach as an essential, invariable feature of the psychiatric discipline, and thus argued that the existence of different theoretical orientations in psychiatry should be regarded not as a flaw and a failing but rather as an evidence of the peculiar integrative nature of the discipline and a consequence of the complexity of the mind and its disorders not only in the case of the mentally ill but also of the sane and healthy individual. As a corollary of this, psychiatric research developed a wide variety of psycho(patho)logical concepts which define the basic mechanisms of – healthy and disturbed – psychic life, and which help to better grasp and describe the genesis and development of the symptoms involved.

To convey a general idea of what was meant by psychopathology as a 'basic science' in the field of psychiatry, I am now going to briefly describe a few of the earlier developed concepts of 'an understanding psychopathology', which altogether do not belong to the category of the psychodynamic concepts, and which nowadays almost no one ever hears about anymore, because they have, on the whole, fallen into oblivion:

Daseinanalysis

Daseinanalysis was first developed by Ludwig Binswanger and Medard Boss. The main goal in daseinanalytical therapy is to make a person's phenomenological world transparent, whereas this transparency leaves the general construct of the original *dasein* intact so as to not have to rebuild a person's being. This construct is subsequently used to be the foundation to analyse the phenomenological world and fix the problems around the already existing existence. This approach was heavily influenced by the German philosopher Martin Heidegger and his existential philosophy. The most reflective proponent of *daseinanalysis* today is Holzhey-Kunz (2002). The intention governing daseinanalysis was to understand psychiatric symptoms of schizophrenia as the expression of an alteration of the structural components of one's own basic being-in-the-world rather than as an abnormality or a 'defect'. The psychotic suffering is thus understood as 'an immediate and radical rebellion against the ontologically determined human existence' (Holzhey-Kunz and Läpple 2008).

Anthropology

The anthropological perspective focusses on the relationship between personality and mental illness. Throughout his entire professional life the German psychiatrist Hubertus Tellenbach (1961) has made major contributions to the study of the pathogenesis of depression. Tellenbach was the first to extensively describe the premorbid and intermorbid personality vulnerable to endogenous depression, whom he called 'typus melancholicus'. This type of personality despairs of his own incapacity to face the ordinary demands and challenges of life and *dasein*. And so the 'typus melancholicus' is characterised by a fixation to order and orderliness, by a peculiar way of having an order and of being in an order, because otherwise he tends to rapidly go downhill (mental illness) in those situations in which that order is under threat. In that sense melancholy is linked to the transformation of movement of life and more specifically to the inhibition of passing of inner life and loss of ground regarding the flow of the world. So one might say, the personality structure of the person vulnerable to melancholia betrays features of a fixation to time and space, a situation that renders the pre-depressive person liable to pass through certain characteristic triggering situations that Tellenbach typifies with the terms *includence* and *remanence* (cf. Ambrosini et al. 2011). The contents of the melancholic delusion (guilt, depletion, health) thus refer *ex negativo* to the central tasks of *dasein* every human being has to come to terms with in his or her life.

Phenomenology and Gestalt psychology

Klaus Conrad (1958) was a German neurologist with important contributions to neuropsychology and psychopathology. In the attempt to broaden the horizon of the understanding of the delusion linked to the complex and central phenomena of schizophrenia, Conrad provided with his stage model of 'Prodomal and beginning Schizophrenia' an impressive description of the early states of schizophrenia from the perspective of the psychology of Gestalt psychology. By proposing that the delusion arises fom an 'already transformed Gestalt perception' wherein the affective and expressive 'holistic' properties of Gestalt become exaggerated, Klaus Conrad challenged the other two existing approaches (i.e. the perspective of the biological psychiatry and that of Binswanger's existential analysis). Conrad coined the term 'Trema' for a behaviour that subsequently turns out to be the forerunner of the onset of schizophrenia and which manifests itself through strange action episodes, which other people consider as irrational behaviour, or as 'crazy action' ('*Unsinnige Handlung*'; Conrad 1958). And since this implies a fundamental break of communication and intersubjectivity, other people perceive the patient's enacted understanding of the world as appearing to be so radically different from their own that they may perceive the patient's deep depression as an unmotivated, strange and irrational act.

At a later stage the patient becomes more and more distrustful and deluded. That's when the first stage, delusional mood (Trema), is superseded by the next stage, apophanic psychosis, which Conrad defined as 'unmotivated seeing of connections accompanied by a specific feeling of abnormal meaningfulness'. Apophany comes from the Geek *apophainesthai* and means 'to become manifest': This is the point in time when the patient finally gives up his reservation of the 'as if', and is firmly convinced that others are able to actually influence his thoughts. This involves perceptual anomalies, as for example misidentification experiences, which means that a stranger, or unfamiliar person, is perceived as known ('misplaced familiarity'). Although the patient, on the one hand, feels omnipotent, on the other he feels threatened, because everything revolves about himself (*anastrophe*): The familiar expressive qualities, arising from the patient's own delusional convictions, from now on emerge from each object he encounters and thus spread with monotonous repetition to his entire field of vision (misplaced familiarity of delusional misidentifications). As a result of this everything becomes overly charged with meaning emitting secret messages.

Finally the stage of apophany is replaced by the apocalyptic stage, which involves the subjective 'reorganisation of meaning' with the view of preserving the subject's 'vital' – albeit now highly delusional – relationship with the world. If the delusion becomes finally irreversible and chronic, the stage of consolidation sets in and prevails (cf. Mishara 2011).

Structural dynamic and affect-logic

Werner Janzarik (1988), one of the great German psychopathologists, was also applying *gestalt* principles to the understanding of schizophrenia. According to Janzarik, psychopathology ensues whenever the balance between structure, i.e. the cognitive representation of the self and the world, and dynamics, i.e. the affective or instinctual motivations and drives, is lost. In his structural-dynamic approach Janzarik postulated that 'dynamic change' was the pathogenic factor in both the affective and the schizophrenic psychoses. For a similar purpose Luc Ciompi (1982) developed his theoretical account of the concept of affect-logic in order to shed light on the interaction between thinking and feeling, that is, between cognition and affect.

Psychiatry, psychopathology, psychodynamics 13

The list could be continued easily, for example with Blankenburg's anthropological analyses of the loss of the natural sense of self-evidence (Blankenburg 1971), or with Glatzel's sociological respectively socio-philosophical concept of 'situation' in psychopathology (Glatzel 1978). What all these approaches have in common is the attempt at understanding and describing the psychological processes of subjective experience which in severe cases may lead to psychotic disorders.

It is not at all surprising but rather symptomatic for psychopathology having lost its status as a basic science, especially if one thinks that today descriptive rating methods like the AMDP system are simply equated with psychopathology (cf. Haug 2002), as if the description of symptoms according to operationalised criteria were the last word on the subject. Against this the psychodynamic approach has not given up the original claim of psychopathology to systematically examine the patient's subjective experience of feeling and thinking and by virtue of this gaining a deeper insight into those processes that underlie the symptoms.

The above-described approaches have one more thing in common: in spite of their importance they all have been more or less forgotten. An 'understanding psychopathology' (Jaspers) has since given way to a purely descriptive psychopathology. And thereby psychopathology has forsaken its most important and prominent task, that is, to try to comprehend the genesis and development of mental disease.

All that remains of these various approaches is the psychodynamic thinking, which to this day insists upon an understanding approach without denying that there are obvious limitations to what can be achieved by way of understanding psychic phenomena. An 'understanding psychopathology' does, of course, not succumb to the mistaken belief that there will be no psychic suffering anymore if only we achieved a complete understanding of the phenomena and processes involved. An understanding psychopathology does not see itself as some offshoot of a metaphysically oriented panpsychism nor is it inclined to ignore the research findings of (neuro)biological sciences. Nevertheless, an understanding psychopathology is primarily person-oriented as it wants to understand and take seriously the mentally ill patient. And so the following questions are of particular relevance:

- How does the patient subjectively experience his illness? How does the patient integrate his 'madness' (*Verrücktheit*) into the whole of his personality structure, no matter what caused the illness initially?
- What are the psychological dispositions responsible for the development of the mental disorder?
- What role do the personality and the life-historical experiences of the patient play in all this?
- How does the patient's personality present itself in the interpersonal encounter? And how must the patient's personality and interpersonality be viewed in relation to each other?

14 Psychiatry, psychopathology, psychodynamics

And so we have to now encounter the crucial question of how we can deal with the issue of personality and interpersonality in psychiatry.

The 'person' of the mentally ill

The criticism levelled at the concept of 'disorder' may be seen as an indication of the limitations of the medicalised and objectifying approach to psychic diseases in general, whereby the person suffering from the illness and his or her personality is not, or not sufficiently, taken into consideration. Michel Foucault (1973) gave a poignant description of the objectifying medical gaze of nineteenth-century medicine that 'penetrates' the patient's body virtually with X-ray eyes in order to finally localise a pathological process in the body's organs and systems. In the course of the last 150 years there have been several attempts to overcome this objectifying approach and instead to introduce some sort of subjectivisation of physiology and medicine, which was accordingly carried out under the motto of 'the introduction of the subject into medicine'. The realisation of the programmatic demand connected with that slogan had been pursued most consistently and consequently by Viktor von Weizsäcker (1950).

It is quite obvious that psychiatry has been more than reluctant to include the concept 'person' into its technical language; and consequently also the term 'personality' is merely referred to in connection with the concept of 'personality *disorder*'. In one of the more recent text books of psychiatry terms like person, subject or identity do not even appear any longer (Müller-Spahn and Gaebel 2002). So it's quite telling that the personality disorders invariably are incorrectly termed as 'dependent personality disorders' instead of 'dependent personality' or 'personality disorder connected with over-dependency'. It seems out of the question to introduce into the technical language of psychiatry a concept of personality that does refer to something other than to pathology as, for instance, to the patient's unique and individual character. One thinks back almost wistfully to Kurt Schneider's definition of psychopathic personalities in his attempt to acknowledge the radically different ways of being in the world that characterises the lifeworld the mentally ill person lives in (Schneider 1980). And this relates particularly to the psychotically ill patient, who had been denied any form of 'personality' for a very long time.

What dimensions are involved when taking into consideration the relevance of the concept of 'person' in the field of psychiatry? Of particular significance here are: subjectivity, individuality and identity. Just to put this point across right from the start: to take seriously the psychotic patient's *subjectivity* cannot be achieved by any intellectual effort alone. What is required for grasping the subjective experiences of the patient is the clinician's emotionally and affectively getting involved with and participating in the patient's idiosyncratic way of experiencing himself/herself and the (inner) world he or she lives in. Although this goes without saying, for the sake of clarity: this approach does radically differ from that of medical or social technology, since any form of *individuality* involves the acceptance of uniqueness and incommensurability. To refer to this cumbersome expression of *incommensurability* in this context here seems to be necessary for the reason that measurability has acquired such a high reputation in a discipline, where experiences that, taken in their individuality, do seem to be so radically unfamiliar or alien and perhaps even beyond the pale of any imaginable form of empathic comprehension that it has now become an established and common practice to measure everything that's individual by the same yard stick, although this method finds itself in complete contradiction with individuality. The philosopher Manfred Frank (1986) pointed out that all what stands out due to a high degree of individuality is not the particular and is not the concrete manifestation of a general rule, but is rather that which transcends the generalising definitions. The involvement with the individuality of another person must therefore necessarily imply a form of empathy that is immediate and spontaneous and essentially non-intellectual. We are made to look at things and people differently only then, if we are able to look at them with a certain amount of curiosity, or even with awe and wonder, because otherwise we will be incapable of accepting and acknowledging their inherent otherness and alienness. To be prepared to accept the concept of *identity* in the field of psychotherapy and psychiatry requires a particular kind of self-reflexivity with regard to one's own world view and idea of man.

At the latest since Otto F. Kernberg has introduced the conceptualisation of the syndrome of identity diffusion, which has a significant bearing on the differential diagnosis and psychotherapy of personality disorders, we are as therapists and clinicians aware of the fact that an identity characterised by rigidity or over-fixation may also be an indication of a more or less severe pathology. In line with this is Dieter Wyss's notion (1973) of 'identity sclerosis', which he found to be a characteristic pathological feature of the melancholic patient. So, the further question would be then: Is the 'flexible man' (Sennett 1998) to be viewed as pathological or is it, on the contrary, precisely the 'mobile man' (Thomä 2002) who is at present considered as the ideal of the perfect and healthy man? The answers to the above questions may turn out very differently and depend on evaluations that – particularly if not made explicit – can have a major effect on the psychotherapeutic process and psychiatric treatment.

A discipline, such as psychiatry, which wants to do justice to the mentally ill person, has to necessarily accept the patient's subjectivity, his unique way of experiencing and being in the world, that is, his individuality, that characterises him/her and may radically differ from our own. The severe aberrations of experience such as those that can, at times, be met with in certain cases of psychosis would seem to represent a particular challenge to the clinician. Any forgetting or not-accepting of this difference may be an obstacle to empathic understanding. And that's why the psychoanalytic approach represents such an essential and vital contribution to psychiatry.

Interpersonality and the 'recognition of the alien'

We continue to encounter the question of what the basic attitude of the clinician or therapist should be when dealing and interacting with the psychotically ill patient. And the further question would be then: how to get involved with the patient in order to take seriously the patient's own unique individuality, subjectivity and identity? It should thus be understood that within such an approach the interpersonal relationship would have to be characterised by a basic attitude that adheres and feels obliged to the formula: 'recognition of the alien'. With regard to the patient's symptoms this formula means that besides the approach that is committed to reifying, medicalising and pathologising the patient and his symptoms, other perspectives should also be permitted and duly taken into consideration. This in turn may lead to conceive of the symptoms not first of all as an index for diagnosis but rather as a manifestation of a form of life with immediate implications for the ways the patient as a human being conducts, for example, his social life. In other words, such an approach would no longer be only about the study of isolated symptoms in view of their clinical (i.e. diagnostic) and aetiological significance, but rather about the understanding of a given type of experience and a given way of being in the world. If one embarks on such a non-pathologising approach it is, of course, possible that for a start it eludes any kind of classification. To have concern for the subject (i.e. for the individual) would thus imply to take due account of the uniqueness of the person which cannot be ordered into or under any general categories; and this in turn necessitates approaching the matter in a particularly intelligent and empathic fashion and to not simply reducing illness and disease to the biological and subpersonal level.

Aside from that, it is essential to consider the cultural influence on the individual person. This brings immediately to mind the fact of the heterogeneity of cultures and the co-existence of a multitude of different foreign forms of living and being in the world. But the expanded perspective of the current discussion necessarily calls for further elucidation, since what happens between different cultures (and between individuals, as it were) cannot be reduced to the simple fact that there are several cultures existing side by side as equals. Let's not be deceived about one basic fact: there is no place beyond cultures that could grant us an unrestrained and unbiased overview, just as there is no place beyond my own self, as it were. Or to put it in other words: we can escape our own culture just as little as we can escape our own identity or our own idiosyncratic way of being and living in the world. And so it is only logical and consistent to beware of imposing specific culture-bound methods upon the other. The 'recognition of the alien' in the person's suffering, in the uniqueness of the individual person, and in the influence of the cultural horizon, all of this could act as a counterbalance to that, which a psychiatry, which is not person-oriented, so urgently needs in order to escape from getting trapped in a pitfall of generalised statements, oversized treatment packages, mechanical rules and policies, and culture-bound, mostly unreflected stereotypes and prejudices.

The 'recognition of the other or the alien' would seem to be the answer to a narrow-mindedness, that is, to a limitedness of thinking, which, firstly, goes on the assumption that there is only one valid point of view, which, secondly, refers only to identities and never to non-identities, and which, thirdly, merely creates views of the world in which there is no place for otherness or alienness; in short, a thinking that conceives of the alien as merely constituting a surpassable lack with the sole purpose of overcoming it and regaining one's old former self. Arguably, all of these designations exhibit a deficit, and there seems to be a complete absence of any kind of confidence in a genuine alien experience, which is to be measured in itself and not just against a putative ideal or possible omnipresence. What we thus need is a shift of weight and a new orientation which opens up new paths. But it is certainly true to say that the alienness, or the alien, will find recognition only then, if it can be accepted as part of one's own identity, because only then can the alien or the other be seen as being not only outside of but also inside of one's self. Such a 'dialectical conceptualisation of personal identity', which is, at the same time, constituted by 'affirmation *and* otherness' was suggested by Gerhard Schneider (1995) a few years ago. In the present discussion it may be sufficient to just briefly make reference to Schneider's line of argumentation in his remarkable and convincing book, which unfortunately has not received a great deal of recognition. What makes Schneider's theoretical discussion so intriguing and worth mentioning in our context here is the fact that he alerts us to a significant difference in the clinician's or therapist's attitude. Following the line of argumentation suggested by Schneider the decisive question arises whether the unfamiliar, the other or alien, is merely conceived as a phenomenon outside ourselves and merely as a disturbing and intrusive element, or whether, on the contrary, it is considered as partly constituting our own identity and our own self and, therefore, is being understood as a necessary and continual expansion and challenge to it.

All this has implications for psychiatry and psychotherapy: it is by far not sufficient that the diagnostic or therapeutic method takes into consideration such problems as the influence of foreign cultures. It rather means that the method approaches and recognises the alien *in toto*, and thus is taking the radicality of alien experience seriously. What's required is a suspension of the assumptions that usually are taken for granted – one might say, what's required is a departure from the familiar, a stepping back in front of the alien or unfamiliar and all that which cannot immediately be appropriated and assimilated, and which also includes the encounter with the culturally alien or unfamiliar, represented by the other person or by the patient. And this designates a basic position or attitude which is absolutely necessary in order to be open and receptive to mental states of delusion, melancholy, suicidal tendency, but incidentally also to multiculturalism, etc. In all of these cases the recognition of the alien is required, whereby three aspects can be said to be most essential:

- the acceptance of the alien, and of all that, which cannot be immediately assimilated and which implies to be prepared to abandon the solid ground of the familiar;
- the curiosity for the alien, which is thus not excluded but rather recognised in its own right and in its meaningfulness for us; and

18 Psychiatry, psychopathology, psychodynamics

- the awareness of one's own alienating defence mechanisms which may be responsible, in first place, for producing that, which is then experienced as alien.

The alienness, which is not responded to and which is not appropriated or worked-through can be said to be presumed as if it were merely a destructive intruder that has to be kept outside. But the same applies, if in the attempt to hastily assimilate the alien, it becomes subjected to premature evaluation and judgement, as a result of which an intellectual quarantine is imposed upon it.

Arguably no other contemporary philosopher has been investigating the *Topographie des Fremden* (*Topography of the Alien*) and *Der Stachel des Fremden* (*The Sting of the Alien*) in more depth and detail than the German phenomenological philosopher Bernhard Waldenfels (1997, 1990). The following quotation could even be viewed as an appropriate description of the required basic attitude of the therapist referred to above, albeit the context the quotation is taken from is a purely philosophical one:

> An experience of the alien understood as something which cannot be pinned down and which is disturbing, enticing or terrifying us by surpassing our expectations and eluding our grasp, affects our own experience in such a way that it turns into a *becoming-alien of experience*. Alienness is self-referential, and it is contagious. Its effects precede any thematisation. . . . This implies [. . .] a fundamental reconsideration and revision of the concept of experience as modernity conceives of it, where it would be seen as a merely subjective feeling. [. . .] An alternative possibility would be to conceive of experience as something which surpasses the limits of self-certainty and thus enters an in-between sphere, where we engage the alien without already neutralizing or denying its effects, its challenges and demands in and through the way of dealing with the alien, the other and unfamiliar [. . .] On this account the immediate experience with its various twists and turns reveals itself as being intrinsically affected by the alien. Experiential orders that disturb the familiar order are integrated into this order by being organized, standardized, classified and normalized, in short, by being filtered out and subjected to explanations, by means of which the alien becomes excluded.
>
> (Waldenfels 1990: 64–65)

The categorisation of mental disorders in psychopathology is precisely based on such an experiential order, which excludes the alien:

> If the pathological in all its forms and manifestations could merely be considered as deficiency, disturbance, impairment or damage, that is, negativity or regressivity, the assessment of what is pathological would be unequivocal: it would merely constitute a surpassable lack or deficit which corresponds to a preliminary state of appropriation of the alien. The underlying logic

operative here is profoundly questionable, because as long as we exclusively and blindly rely upon this logic we fail to see that it comes at the price of denying and violating the very alien experience from which every empowerment begins. [. . .] Diverging from an existing order, which takes us outside ourselves and which lets us transcend the boundaries of the specific existing order, may then be experienced as simply otherness and difference and not as mere chaos or non-order.

(Waldenfels 1990: 70)

It would therefore appear necessary to apply dialectical thinking in psychopathology and, in addition to that, to bring dialectic thinking beyond psychopathology up to human existence itself for the purpose of explaining how difficult it is for all of us to achieve a viable conception of personal identity. We have to advance the dialectic perspective in order to (re-)connect seeming opposites that manifest themselves in different ways, such as: affirmation and otherness (cf. G. Schneider), exclusion of the alien and appropriation of the alien. However, to deny what is negative in the symptom (the abnormality or illness) and to exclusively see the positive aspects of it, this would amount to negating its alien character. And yet this seemed to have been the crucial error of the so-called anti-psychiatry movement. Even if we assume that there is method and meaning in madness, it still remains madness or *Verrücktheit*. The dialectical character becomes particularly evident in the attempt of the appropriation of the alien. And since the alien can never be resolved entirely, it is particularly difficult to bear and tolerate this still ever-present dialectical tension. Viewed from this perspective the anti-psychiatry movement *and* its counter tendencies, as for example represented by the so-called biological psychiatry, do not fundamentally differ from each other, since the biological psychiatry as well as its opponent both endeavoured – even if it may be for very different reasons – to eliminate what appeared to them as alien. If a mental disturbance is considered as purely biologically caused, and not seen in any way to be linked to the patient's subjectivity – perhaps at the most reluctantly admitted to impact on it – then this perspective undoubtedly clouds our perception of what the alien could mean for the constitution of our self and our self-identity: exclusively viewed as the result of neuronal and synaptic malfunctioning the psychopathological phenomena are deprived of any significant and meaningful properties.

A 'person-oriented psychiatry', on the other hand, depends and lives on the dialectical tension between: classification *and* the person's singularity and uniqueness; the methodically well-thought-out approach to the patient's mental suffering *and* the subjectivity of the person suffering from mental illness; the intention of effecting a cure *and* the recognition of suffering and illness in all its various forms and manifestations. So the crucial question would be then: what does an understanding psychiatry look like if it is to avoid a unilateral and generalising approach to human suffering? Does psychiatry become completely absorbed in objectifying thinking *or* is it still capable of taking the subject's personality and singularity into account? Does psychiatry tend to generalise its own method *or* is it capable of self-critically acknowledging its own limitations; and finally, is psychiatry only interested in the pathological aspects of the symptom *or* is it willing to recognise and acknowledge the more creative, healthy, original and inventive aspects of the symptom as well? Now, these are opposites that manifest themselves in different ways: either in a 'this as well as that', (which is characteristic of the application of dialectical thinking), or else in a choice of 'either–or'. The introduction and advancement of the dialectic perspective into psychiatry will be – beyond empirical data – a criterion for and an indication of the efficiency and quality of the various psychiatric and psychotherapeutic approaches.

The psychoanalytical approach can raise the claim to be the one method that can better than any other method provide the theoretical and clinical prerequisites for 'the recognition of the alien'. Self-reflexivity is inherent to the psychoanalytic method. And one can say that the dialectical character of the therapeutic situation is evidenced by the fact that the clinician or therapist time and again scrutinises his own experience of the patient's subjective experiences and in doing so tacitly recognises the need to acknowledge that the lifeworld inhabited by the patient is not like his own. Psychoanalysis is thus essentially concerned with the subject (i.e. with the individual, his singularity and uniqueness). And this above all explains and justifies the – in most cases – extended duration of the psychoanalytic treatment. The individual case bears fundamental significance for the provision of unique possibilities of otherwise unattainable new insights which expand and go beyond any existing theoretical horizon, as the encounter between two personalities is always a significant and singular event. But because the encounter with the psychotically ill person is often an unexpected, unpredictable and incalculable event, these above-described essential qualities and abilities, required of the clinician or therapist, will inevitably be put to a severe test. The main part of this book will focus upon the various meaning-oriented and contextually sensitive approaches that have been developed in the course of the history of psychoanalysis and that have considerably contributed to the understanding of psychotic phenomena and the treatment of psychotic patients.

Chapter 2

Psychoanalytic theories about psychosis

In the following discussion two different approaches in dealing with the subject are proposed and examined in relation to one another: the historical approach and the systematic one. As so often in psychoanalytic writing, the account in this chapter takes its point of departure from Sigmund Freud's original theoretical contributions; in this case from his conceptions of psychosis to then take account of the various developments after Freud. The historical approach does not serve an end in itself, though, but rather serves as a means for the purpose of being able to examine Freud's early psychoanalytic conceptualisations with regard to the extent to which they can still today contribute to the understanding of psychoses.

Psychosis as a defensive process and a remodelling of reality (according to Freud)

At the beginning of the twentieth century psychiatric research was focussed primarily upon the issue of delusion. Delusion was for a very long time regarded as the quintessence of madness (*Verrücktheit*). Psychotic experiences like delusions were considered as incomprehensible and inaccessible to empathic understanding and consequently it was commonly believed that delusion is a somatogenic disease. Against this background it seems only logical that psychoanalysis in its attempt to understand the psychotically ill individual first of all focussed its efforts on the analysis of delusion as a psychogenic disease.

Delusion as a projection of instinctual wishes

In its beginnings psychoanalysis was a psychology of the drives which had set itself the task of exploring the vicissitudes of the drives; and so this applied to its investigation of psychosis as well. It is worthwhile, even today, to study Freud's classical papers on this issue. They are not only of relevance from a historical point of view as will be demonstrated further below. Freud's study of the Schreber case was undeniably a pioneering achievement: after reading Daniel Paul Schreber's book *Memoirs of My Nervous Illness* (Schreber 2000; first published in 1903) Freud published his own analysis of Schreber eight years later in 'Psychoanalytic Notes

22 Psychoanalytic theories about psychosis

on an Autobiographical Account of a Case of Paranoia (Dementia Paranoides)' (Freud 1911).

Freud in his Schreber study developed two important psychoanalytic concepts that are still relevant today. Freud interpreted Schreber's delusion as a projection, which meant that he did not consider delusion as an incomprehensible and inaccessible but as a psychologically determined phenomenon. Freud understood delusion as an attempt at restitution, a process of reconstruction. And this actually amounts to a transvaluation of delusion: the delusional formation which had so far been taken to be merely a pathological product is, according to Freud, in reality to be seen as an attempt at recovery. Both ideas will be dealt with in more depths in what follows.

Where psychiatry saw obviously only biological forces at work, Freud postulated a psychological mechanism, even before the development and outbreak of delusional psychosis. Freud describes this mechanism as projection. According to Freud, the cause of paranoia is to be found in Schreber's repressed homosexuality. The reasons why it had to be repressed are due to the spirit of the age (*zeitgeist*), to the discrimination and criminalisation of homosexuals, but furthermore to unresolved unconscious conflicts with the powerful figure of the father. The passive homosexual wishful phantasy initially directed towards the father is then owed to a process of displacement and projection transferred on to other persons, at first, Dr Flechsig, who was the physician and psychiatrist in charge. But as the delusion of persecution further develops, the figure of Flechsig is replaced by the superior figure of God, who in Schreber's delusional world demands Schreber's transformation into a woman.

> We shall therefore, I think, raise no further objections to the hypothesis that the exciting cause of the illness was the appearance in him of a feminine (that is, a passive homosexual) wishful phantasy, which took as its object the figure of his doctor. An intense resistance to this phantasy arose on the part of Schreber's personality, and the ensuing defensive struggle, which might perhaps just as well have assumed some other shape, took on, for reasons unknown to us, that of a delusion of persecution. The person he longed for now became his persecutor, and the content of his wishful phantasy became the content of his persecution. It may be presumed that the same schematic outline will turn out to be applicable to other cases of delusions of persecution.
> (Freud 1911: 47)

What is noteworthy in this quotation is the fact that Freud, firstly, seems to make no fundamental difference between neurosis and psychosis (he writes: 'which might perhaps just as well have assumed some other shape') and that he, secondly, suggests a process of defence as a characteristic component of the psychotic mechanism. But if one takes the view that what lies at the core of psychosis is a defence strategy, does this not imply that there must be an active ego, a shaping force informing the psychotic experience?

Psychoanalytic theories about psychosis 23

In the further course of his study of the Schreber case, Freud focusses on the drive destiny of Schreber's passive homosexual phantasy. Freud emphasises that one should be careful about drawing general inferences from a single type of paranoia. And Freud is also quite aware of the fact that the view that the homosexual phantasy lies at the core of the conflict in cases of paranoia might cause offense to some of his readers. But this did not keep him from providing a precise and detailed explanation of the various permutations of the wishful phantasy, which under the rod of defence goes through all sorts of contortions and alterations.

Nevertheless, it is a remarkable fact that the familiar principal forms of paranoia can all be represented as contradictions of the single proposition: '*I* (a man) *love him* (a man)', and indeed that they exhaust all the possible ways in which such contradictions could be formulated.

The proposition 'I (a man) love him' is contradicted by: (a) Delusions of *persecution*, for they loudly assert: 'I do not *love* him – I *hate* him.' This contradiction, which must have run thus in the unconscious, cannot, however, become conscious to the paranoiac in this form. The mechanism of symptom-formation in paranoia requires that internal perceptions – feelings – shall be replaced by external perceptions. Consequently the proposition 'I hate him' becomes transformed by *projection* into another one: '*He hates* (persecutes) *me*, which will justify me in hating him.' And thus the impelling unconscious feeling makes its appearance as though it were the consequence of an external perception: 'I do not *love* him – I *hate* him, because HE PERSECUTES ME.' [. . .] (b) Another element is chosen for contradiction in *erotomania*, which remains totally unintelligible on any other view: 'I do not love *him* – I love *her*.' And in obedience to the same need for projection, the proposition is transformed into: 'I observe that *she* loves me.' 'I do not love *him* – I love *her*, because SHE LOVES ME.' [. . .] c) The third way in which the original proposition can be contradicted would be delusions of *jealousy*, which we can study in the characteristic forms in which they appear in each sex. [. . .] If now these men become the objects of a strong libidinal cathexis in his unconscious, he will ward it off with the third kind of contradiction: 'It is not *I* who love the man – *she* loves him', and he suspects the woman in relation to all the men whom he himself is tempted to love. [. . .]

Now it might be supposed that a proposition consisting of three terms, such as '*I love him*', could only be contradicted in three different ways. Delusions of jealousy contradict the subject, delusions of persecution contradict the verb, and erotomania contradicts the object. But in fact a fourth kind of contradiction is possible – namely, one which rejects the proposition as a whole: '*I do not love at all – I do not love anyone*.' And since, after all, one's libido must go somewhere, this proposition seems to be the psychological equivalent of the proposition: 'I love only myself.' So that this kind of contradiction would give us megalomania, which we may regard as a *sexual overvaluation of the ego* . . .

(Freud 1911: 63–65)

24 Psychoanalytic theories about psychosis

This is indeed a striking description, which Freud offers here. The defence can attach to each single element of a propositional sentence (i.e. of the common statement form). The grammatical references (i.e. the relation of subject–predicate–object) is continually confounded. At this point we are already close to the realisation that psychotic experiences invariably entail a change in the use of language, that is, not a loss of language but rather a manipulation of it. But if the defences have already a profound effect on the basic thought processes, then this may have unforeseeable consequences for the future development, because the thinking capacity as such is already significantly affected and impaired.

Freud's study of the Schreber case is entirely based on the drive psychological approach of the early days of psychoanalysis which is no longer considered as being of great relevance for psychoanalysis today. Paranoia is no longer conceived of as the result of a projection of repressed homosexual wishes. Furthermore, we have to note that today we as clinicians have to pay particular attention to the quality of the patient's early as well as current relationships and experiences, and to the patient's mental structure with its various deficits but also its potential. Although viewed from a historical perspective Freud's study on Schreber can be said to be a pioneering achievement in the history of psychoanalysis, we as contemporary clinicians have, at the same time, to ask ourselves, whether it still bears relevance for today's clinical practice. And indeed the answer to be given to this question is that there are several aspects that may even nowadays provide the clinician with useful insights:

- The projection of inner experiences or wishes on to the exterior world is still a valid concept for the understanding of the genesis and development of a delusional disorder. But it is rather the development of paranoia than the schizophrenic-psychotic disorders for which this specific defence mechanism provides a useful explanation and important understanding.
- The significance of sexuality and sexual conflicts is still insufficiently taken into consideration for the development of psychotic disorders. Only in severe cases of sexual violence and abuse its relevance is acknowledged.

The influence of early incestuous fixations to a parent on the part of the child that later in life develops a psychotic condition can be frequently encountered in clinical practice. The development of such an incestuous fixation may be due to manifest seduction or else it may be the outcome of an overall incestuous atmosphere where boundaries are constantly disregarded and violated. A clinical example may illustrate this:

Mrs R. is a 62-year-old woman with a paranoid symptomatology, which is directed towards her husband with whom she has been living for several decades now. Their marriage displays a specific dynamic: her husband regularly demonstrates his superiority and plays out his strengths by bossing her around and 'keeping her in leading-strings', whereas she can't help but letting herself be patronised. She seems incapable of standing up to him and thus swallows a lot and holds in whatever comes to her mind. And so she doesn't really say anything to her husband about what's bothering her almost all of the time.

About every two years her always latently present delusion seizes hold of her and gets the upper hand. She is persuaded that her husband is after her blood and seeks to kill her. She is convinced that behind her back there is a pally relationship going on between her husband and some other man. What she hears from what her husband says more or less allusively, becomes increasingly an *idée fixe* and later finds its way into her daily life to then eventually take over her mind completely: Although her husband tries to cover up this chumminess, she firmly believes that behind her back there are secret and collusive arrangements going on between her husband and this other man. She becomes ever more suspicious against her husband, and so tries to keep out of his way.

So the question has to be raised: What exactly is it that disturbs her extremely fragile and precarious equilibrium and regularly throws her off balance? Whenever sexual desires are awakened in her, which she neither is able to integrate nor to otherwise adequately deal with, the delusion breaks out and the delusional beliefs start taking over her life. And the other question would be: To whom could she address her sexual wishes? Whom could she choose as her love-object? Her husband? Given the ongoing marital problems with her husband, this didn't seem possible, because then her sexual wishes would have come into irreconcilable conflict with her accumulated feelings of hate towards her husband due to his dominating over her for all of these years and even decades. Or perhaps choose another man? This would run counter to her inner working model of the submissive and obedient wife, and amount to a transgression of the 'no-go areas' of self-realisation and self-expression. But, on the other hand, she is a vigorous woman. And even at her age, just in her early sixties, she still has got a lively and vivacious personality and is always receptive and open to her own wishes and desires.

The further question would be then: How could the patient be helped in therapy? My interpretations seem to gradually begin to fall on fertile ground: she is rather open to the tentative interpretations I make, and she also does not reject the idea that there might be a connection between the deterioration of her state of mental health and her sexual wishes. But in the very next breath she insists that it is absolutely certain that the actual reality is just the way as she perceives and experiences it – so that it strikes me as highly improbable that I really had managed to reach her.

But then something very remarkable happens: On the psychiatric ward at the hospital, where she is currently being treated, there is another fellow female patient who is about the same age and just about as helpless as Mrs R. herself. She obviously seeks the proximity to this woman: She shows solidarity with this particular fellow patient, helps her in whatever way, and she can be seen all day

26 Psychoanalytic theories about psychosis

long walking around accompanied by this other woman. And to everyone's astonishment Mrs R. finds a new lease of life and the delusion seems to have disappeared all of a sudden. This gives rise to the assumption that all what counts for Mrs R. is to express her solidarity with *another woman,* who might in turn help her regain some sort of identity feeling *as* a woman.

The clinical example conveys a clear idea of the patient's fixation to her early love objects which later in her life she finds very difficult to impute to her husband. And so the only solution open to her seems to deny and ward off her own instinctual impulses and sexual wishes, a situation which can be considered as an important stress factor, albeit presumably not the only one, responsible for the onset of the patient's psychotic episode and her delusional experiences.

Delusion as 'weltenaufgang'

Then, a further question must have imposed itself on Sigmund Freud: what lies at the core of the psychotic condition? Are there particular organic and biological factors under which influence psychotic illness may develop? This is a question psychiatry has always been concerned with. At the time, when Freud worked on the Schreber case, the situation was such that in the professional circles of psychiatry the general opinion prevailed that the patient's psychotic and delusional experiences are not comprehensible via the clinician's standard empathic capacities and are therefore to be viewed as basically the product of biological processes. And this is precisely the point, where Freud brought in a completely new and antithetical idea: Freud's revolutionary discovery was that before the onset of the delusional episode, the patient withdraws the libidinal cathexis from the objects of the external world and directs it on to the ego. Accordingly, the psychotic delusion has to be conceived of as the second step in this process, as some kind of *weltenaufgang,* after the world, as the patient previously knew it, has come to an end. And this justifies the conclusion that the delusional formation is in reality an attempt at recovery, a process of reconstruction, and an attempt at recapturing a relation to the people and things in the world:

> A world-catastrophe of this kind is not infrequent during the agitated stage in other cases of paranoia. If we base ourselves on our theory of libidinal cathexis, and if we follow the hint given by Schreber's view of other people as being 'cursorily improvised men', we shall not find it difficult to explain these catastrophes. The patient has withdrawn from the people in his environment and from the external world generally the libidinal cathexis which he has hitherto directed unto them. Thus everything has become indifferent and irrelevant to him, and has to be explained by means of a secondary rationalization as being 'miracled up, cursorily improvised'. The end of the world is the projection of his internal catastrophe; his subjective world has come to an end since his withdrawal of his love from it. [. . .]

And the paranoiac builds it again, not more splendid, it is true, but at least so that he can once more live in it. He builds it up by the work of his delusions. *The delusional formation, which we take to be the pathological product, is in reality an attempt at recovery, a process of reconstruction.* Such a reconstruction after the catastrophe is successful to a greater or lesser extent, but never wholly so; in Schreber's words, there has been a 'profound internal change' in the world. But the human subject has recaptured a relation, and often a very intense one, to the people and things in the world, even though the relation is a hostile one now, where formerly it was affectionate. We may say, then, that the process of repression proper consists in a detachment of the libido from people – and things – that were previously loved. It happens silently; we receive no intelligence of it, but can only infer it from subsequent events. What forces itself so noisily upon our attention is the process of recovery, which undoes the work of repression and brings back the libido again on the people it had abandoned.

(Freud 1911: 69–71)

This conceptualisation was an outstanding achievement that demonstrates Freud's genius. So, according to him, what resides at the core of psychosis are not primarily the patient's delusional and mad (*ver-rückt*) beliefs and ideas, but rather the patient's endeavours to re-build by the work of his delusions the world after the catastrophe occurred, whereby it can, of course, never come to a really successful and satisfactory outcome. So, in following Freud's line of thinking we now can see that at the beginning there is a disruption of relationship, an emotional withdrawal from other people. In the terminology of drive psychology, one would say that the point of departure is 'the detachment of the libido from people that were previously loved'. By the work of his delusion the patient seeks to then bring back the libido again on to the people it had abandoned, though naturally without being wholly successful in it.

Narcissism versus object relationship in psychosis

The next question will concern the specific quality of object-cathexes of the psychotic patient. If the psychotically ill person through his projections manages, to a certain extent at least, to recapture a relationship to the people and things in the world, that is, if it is true that the delusion is basically a re-building of the world, we then continue to encounter the question of how viable this re-engagement with the world really is, and especially how good it is at building up relationships upon it. Here Freud seems to be rather pessimistic, particularly with regard to the therapeutic technique and the patient's presumed incapacity to be accessible to therapeutic efforts.

The concept of 'narcissism' that Freud developed in 1914 (Freud 1914), once again highlights the psychotic patient's withdrawal of the libido from the external objects and its subsequent retreat into the ego. Characteristic for primary narcissism

28 Psychoanalytic theories about psychosis

is, according to Freud, that the ego takes itself as its own love object, which implies that the libidinal object-cathexes have been given up. In 1915 then Freud postulates in his paper 'The Unconscious' (Freud 1915) that psychotic patients, for whom narcissistic self-love and impaired object-cathexis due to the repudiation of the external world is characteristic, are unsuitable for psychoanalytic treatment, because they are incapable of developing a transference relationship.

> In the case of schizophrenia, on the other hand, we have been driven to the assumption that after the process of repression the libido that has been withdrawn does not seek a new object, but retreats into the ego; that is to say, that here the object-cathexes are given up and a primitive objectless condition of narcissism is re-established. The incapacity of these patients for transference (so far as the pathological process extends), their consequent inaccessibility to therapeutic efforts, their characteristic repudiation of the external world, the appearance of signs of a hypercathexis of their own ego, the final outcome in complete apathy – all these clinical features seem to agree excellently with the assumption that their object-cathexes have been given up.
>
> (Freud 1915: 196–197)

The theory of narcissism seems to be particularly suited for comprehending and describing the psychotic patient's withdrawal into his own world, his inaccessibility, his autism (cf. Bleuler 1911). But in the past the theory of narcissism unfortunately also contributed to the situation of not undertaking psychotherapy with psychotic patients, or at most with little hope of a successful outcome of the treatment. The alleged absence of the transference seemed to usher in the farewell – fortunately only temporarily – of the psychotherapeutic treatment of psychoses. What's more, the theory of narcissism leaves several important questions open: What role plays destructiveness in the genesis and development of psychosis? What are the motivations for withdrawing the libido from the outside world? Can the reason for this perhaps be traced back to past painful relationship experiences? Or put differently: If the withdrawal of the libido was not actually an attempt at reconstruction, then maybe at least an attempt at self-rescue, when early in life the significant others came too close or were felt to be intrusive? This considered, is the retreat into the ego (i.e. the state of narcissism) perhaps to be conceived of as a defence mechanism, as a mental strategy for the purpose of defending the self against destructive over-proximity? And what is the specific function of the object that has become the target of massive projections? Even though it is, strictly speaking, not a libidinal cathexis of the object, the object remains more than ever a focus of attention, if the psychotic patient feels persecuted by it – so what is it then that the psychotically ill person wants from the object?

And thus we can see that these questions bring to light some of the weak areas of the libido theory, which is obviously not suitable for identifying the exact quality and functionality of the object. And indeed, the libido theory is primarily concerned with the economy of instinctual cathexes and thus merely distinguishes

Psychoanalytic theories about psychosis 29

between object-cathexis or the withdrawal of object-cathexis. Given the fact that with Freud's libido theory the investigation of the quality of the object relations is too narrowly considered, it should come as no surprise that Melanie Klein and her followers would not strictly hold on to the libido concept, but would instead complement and expand it and subsequently develop new ideas and conceptualisations especially with the aim of exploring the nature of object-relationships.

Psychotic language and the return to the object

Whereas Freud in his paper on the Schreber case was still dealing with the paranoid mechanisms analogous to those mechanisms met with in cases of neurosis, he then began to ask himself very soon whether it is really appropriate to hypothesise a similar psychic mechanism in cases of neurosis and psychosis. After all, the mode of psychic experience and the prospect of a successful treatment result appeared to be so very different. And besides, one issue remains to be resolved: If it is true that the *weltenaufgang* entails a return to the object, then why should the development of a transference in psychotherapy not be possible? In what way does the psychotic patient succeed, and in what way does he fail in his attempt to return to the object, that is, in his attempt to recapture a relation to the object by the work of his delusions? This still awaits a more detailed explanation and closer definition. We shall be in a position to answer both of these questions, after we have taken a closer look at the schizophrenic patient's peculiarities of speech, since this will help us to elucidate an essential aspect, which is extremely relevant for our further discussion. In 1915 Freud wrote in his paper 'The Unconscious':

> In schizophrenics we observe – especially in the initial stages, which are so obstructive – a number of changes in *speech,* some of which deserve to be regarded from a particular point of view. The patient often devotes peculiar care to his way of expressing himself, which becomes 'stilted' and 'precious'. The construction of his sentences undergoes a peculiar disorganization, making them so incomprehensible to us that his remarks seem nonsensical. Some reference to bodily organs and innervations is often given prominence in the content of these remarks. This may be added to the fact that in such symptoms of schizophrenia as are comparable with the substitutive formations of hysteria or obsessional neurosis, the relation between the substitute and the repressed material nevertheless displays peculiarities which would surprise us in these two forms of neurosis.
>
> (Freud 1915: 197)

The first idea – as he points out explicitly in his paper (ibid.) – Freud owes to Viktor Tausk, to whom we will return in more detail further below. Tausk's original idea, and even more so Freud's comprehensive consideration of it, is quite remarkable and concerns the following question: Is it an indication of psychotic experience if the patient is overly conscious of the processes of the body and its organs,

30   Psychoanalytic theories about psychosis

whereby these processes assume a very specific and extraordinary meaning for the patient? Freud's second idea concerns the distinction between neurosis and psychosis. And so we will see in what way the patient's relation to language can be indicative of it being a case of neurosis or psychosis.

If we ask ourselves what it is that gives the character of strangeness to the substitutive formation and the symptom in schizophrenia, we eventually come to realize that it is the predominance of what has to do with words over what has to do with things. [. . .]

If we now put this finding alongside the hypothesis that in schizophrenia object-cathexes are given up, we shall be obliged to modify the hypothesis by adding that the cathexis of the *word*-presentation of objects is retained. What we have permissibly called the conscious presentation of the object can now be split up into the presentation of the *word* and the presentation of the *thing*; the latter consists in the cathexis, if not of the direct memory-images of the thing, at least of remoter memory-traces derived from these. We now seem to know all at once what the difference is between a conscious and an unconscious presentation. The two are not, as we supposed, different registrations of the same content in different psychical localities, nor yet different functional states of cathexis in the same locality; but the conscious presentation comprises the presentation of the thing plus the presentation of the word belonging to it, while the unconscious presentation is the presentation of the thing alone. [. . .] Now, too, we are in a position to state precisely what it is that repression denies to the rejected presentation in the transference-neuroses: what it denies to the presentation is translation into words which shall remain attached to the object. A presentation which is not put into words, or a psychical act which is not hypercathected, remains thereafter in the *Ucs.* in a state of repression. [. . .]

As regards schizophrenia, which we only touch on here so far as seems indispensable for a general understanding of the *Ucs.*, a doubt must occur to us whether the process here termed repression has anything at all in common with the repression which takes place in the transference neuroses. [. . .]

If, in schizophrenia, this flight consists in withdrawal of instinctual cathexis from the points which represent the *unconscious* presentation of the object, it may seem strange that the part of the presentation of this object which belongs to the system *Pcs.* – namely the word-presentations corresponding to it – should, on the contrary, receive a more intense cathexis. We might rather expect that the word-presentation, being the preconscious part, would have to sustain the first impact of repression and that it would be totally uncathectable after repression had proceeded as far as the unconscious thing-presentations. This, it is true, is difficult to understand. It turns out that the cathexis of the word-presentation is not part of the act of repression, but represents the first of the attempts at recovery or cure which so conspicuously dominate the clinical picture of schizophrenia. These endeavours are directed towards regaining the lost object, and it may well be that to achieve this purpose they set off on a path that leads to the object via the verbal part of it, but then find themselves obliged to be content with words instead of things.

(Freud 1915: 196–204)

The distinction between 'word-presentation' and 'thing-presentation' is a conception that first made it possible for Freud to retrace and thus explain the mental mechanisms at work that allow the schizophrenic to recapture a relation to the object and yet, at the same time, retain the withdrawal of libido cathexis from it. Libidinal de-cathexis takes place by a mode of mental operation, by way of which the relations of words to the unconscious thing-presentations are given up. In order to subsequently find his way back to the object, the schizophrenic individual starts to treat concrete things as though they were words, which implies that the words are 'over-cathected'.

This has serious and far-reaching consequences. Thinking in abstractions or in word formations, which normally constitutes a viable link or passage between word and object, may involve the danger of neglecting the relations of words to the unconscious thing-presentations. If this is actually the case, words are no longer treated as though they were something abstract. Instead words are now treated as though they were real, concrete things. Words and things are equated, a situation which ushers in a change of mode of mental operation characteristic of the schizophrenic, commonly described as concrete thinking. Yet, if the word is charged with the 'reality content' of the thing itself, thoughts may become frightening, overwhelming or even persecuting. Language is deprived of its typical 'as-if' character. However, if language no longer serves the function of creating a vital and emotional, or even passionate link between word and object, then the schizophrenic patient must bring to bear ever more and more words, but, naturally, to no avail.

With his meta-psychological paper 'The Unconscious' Freud made a key contribution to the understanding of the psychoses, in that he paid particular attention to the schizophrenic patient's relation to language. And thus Freud paved the way for all those psychoanalysts who, after Freud, took a special interest in the psychotic's peculiarities of speech, that is, his specific relation to language. In this context Hanna Segal (1957) and Jacques Lacan (2006) deserve to be given pride of place.

The concrete thinking of the schizophrenic and the incapacity to symbolise

Freud in his various conceptualisations did in principle already anticipate what some psychoanalysts after him further developed and elaborated, while most of these psychoanalytic authors after Freud were, at the same time, drawing on modern linguistic theories. Hanna Segal (1957), for her part, emphasised the difference between symbolism proper and symbolic equation in which the symbol is equated

32 Psychoanalytic theories about psychosis

with the original object, giving rise to concrete thinking. With this she made a major contribution to psychoanalytic theory which she deservedly became famous for. According to Segal, a characteristic feature of the psychotic patient is his failure to symbolise: symbolic equation takes the place of proper symbols. The capacity to form and use symbols is only possible on the basis of accepting that psychic reality and external reality are not identical. But if this differentiation cannot be made, the object (i.e. the symbol) becomes confused with the mental content of the subject, in other words, with the meaning the subject wants to symbolise. Meaning and symbol become identical, and, therefore, the symbol becomes the thing symbolised, which Hanna Segal termed symbolic equation and which she contrasted with symbol-formation proper. In any case, if symbols are exactly the thing they symbolise, this produces serious effects on the individual's capacity to think, a situation or state of affairs we shall now try to shed some more light upon by making a detour via linguistic theory.

The capacity to use and understand language is based on a fundamental property of language: its metaphorical function. Metaphor derives from the Greek *metaphorá*, which means 'transfer'. Metaphor is a figure of speech that refers to one thing by mentioning another thing. There are plenty of examples of daily metaphors we use, such as: 'to have a heart for others'. In this expression heart is a metaphor for love and affection. And thus, it can be said, language itself is based on the metaphorical function. Each single word signifies (or refers to) an object which is not identical with it. There is always a difference, an interval, between word and object.

Since the linguist and semiologist Charles S. Peirce (1983) we know that things are even more complicated and complex than that. The sign refers to a signified and both refer to a real object: the referent. If we apply this triadic function of the sign to object-relationships, then we have to say that first there is a reference person, for example, the female partner (referent), who is loved in a particular way (signified), an emotion which then can be given expression to by making use of a word (signifier): 'love'. But no single word can stand for itself: the word (signifier) assumes only meaning in reference to other words (signifiers), that is, when referring to or standing for something other than itself. A word has a particular meaning because of its difference from the words that surround it. The central idea is that the meaning of a word is determined within an entire system of oppositional and contrastive relationships. It was the linguist Ferdinand de Saussure (1916) who emphasised this referential context of the signifiers.

The capacity to use language basically depends on a double difference and the negations involved. First, there is the difference between signifier (word) and signified (thing), which implies the negation of the reality character of the words as well as the negation of reality as something completely knowable. And then there is the difference of signifiers from other signifiers, which implies the negation of the absolutely perfect and 'redeeming' word.

Hanna Segal holds the view that in the symbolic equation the symbol becomes the real thing for the psychotic patient. In that case words can literally move mountains. And it also means: lies or excuses do not exist. The lover's oath cannot be put in a relative perspective. The confession 'I love you utterly and completely' becomes all encompassing, from which there seems to be no escape any more. If the partner 'loves you to bits and to pieces', then she is becoming a menace to the person she loves, because such a form of love does not only lay claim to the other person's self-determination but even to the other person's life.

> Mrs W. suffers from severe depression. In the course of her depression she develops different forms of psychotic experience, such as hallucinations and other psychotic problems. Among the most prominent of these symptoms is the olfactory reference syndrome. Mrs W. is obsessed with the idea of emitting abnormal and foul body odours, especially when she is taking off her shoes. And so she thinks she has to keep for herself and, as a corollary of this, avoids any contact with other people. During her long inpatient stay at the clinic she is frequently encouraged to take up contact and communicate with other patients. But she strictly refuses. Since she is absolutely convinced that other people are thinking that 'something stinks about her', she firmly believes that any attempt at making contact with others would be foredoomed to failure.
>
> That 'we stink to others' from time to time, or that 'others stink to us' from time to time, is a common German idiom. If the metaphor is taken literally, though, then the smell or stink, i.e. the thing, is literally inscribed into and onto the body. The loss of the metaphorical function produces a hallucinatory belief – a figure of speech turns into a perceptual belief.

Unless we are not able to play with words and instead take them to be as real concrete things, we shall not be up to the task of making use of words in a meaningful, useful and creative way, but have to only get rid of them. These or similar ideas have inspired the work of a number psychoanalysts and psychoanalytic writers, who have taken over the legacy of Sigmund Freud, and who in their unwavering efforts to find new therapeutic approaches which would especially help the psychotic patient, whose impediment of thought could at times be so severe that they were practically incapable of thinking their own thoughts, developed a wide range of new and innovative theoretical and clinical concepts. The most famous among those analysts concerned with developing new theories of psychoses, are the psychoanalysts Jacques Lacan and Wilfred R. Bion. There are many others, who would also be worth mentioning, but it would go beyond the scope of this discussion. One thing is certain: the therapeutic goal was to help the psychotic patients to find a way to deal with their thoughts other than in a concrete and unplayful manner, and possibly even help them develop a mental capacity to digest and process their previously non-digestible thoughts.

The psychotic person's approach to reality

What's most characteristic for the psychotic disorders is the loss of reality. Self and other are confused and cannot be experienced as separate from each other.

34   Psychoanalytic theories about psychosis

In a state of delusion the other person is invariably experienced as intrusive and persecutory. And thereby the deluded subject may have lost touch with reality to such an extent that other people cannot even remotely understand or relate to these persecutory fears. The structural model, which Freud introduced in 1923 in his work *The Ego and the Id* (1923), and in which Freud proposed a differentiation of the mental apparatus, on the basis of which the psychodynamic and interdependent relationships between the ego, the id, the superego and external reality could be represented and described in a simple and perspicuous manner, also allowed Freud to now formulate and describe in more detail new ideas and insights in view of the relevant question of the difference between neurosis and psychosis.

The decisive factor in psychosis is the creation of a new reality, after the old reality has been disavowed and given up: This means that in psychosis reality is gradually remodelled by the work of the delusions. By contrast, in neurosis reality is accepted but is, at the same time, avoided. On the basis of the mechanisms of defence the conflicting instinctual impulses are repressed, and due to the now unconscious instinctual demands of the id the repressed material struggles against this fate of frustration and unfulfilment and forces itself upon the ego by way of symptoms and compromise formations. Unlike in neurosis, in psychosis reality is not accepted.

> Both neurosis and psychosis are thus the expression of a rebellion on the part of the id against the external world, of its unwillingness – or, if one prefers, its incapacity – to adapt itself to the exigencies of reality, to 'ananke' or necessity. Neurosis and psychosis differ from each other far more in their first, introductory, reaction than in the attempt at reparation which follows it.
>
> Accordingly, the initial difference is expressed thus in the final outcome: in neurosis a piece of reality is avoided by a sort of flight, whereas in psychosis it is remodelled. Or we might say: in psychosis, the initial flight is succeeded by an active phase of remodelling; in neurosis, the initial obedience is succeeded by a deferred attempt at flight. Or again, expressed in yet another way: neurosis does not disavow the reality, it only ignores it; psychosis disavows it and tries to replace it.
>
> (Freud 1924: 185)

Freud in his paper 'The Loss of Reality in Neurosis and Psychosis' (ibid.) continues to describe the fundamental difference in the subject's mode of adaptation to reality in neurosis and in psychosis. In neurosis, Freud implies, the subject is trying to change himself, that is, the internal environment, which Freud refers to as autoplastic adaptation. In psychosis the subject is trying to change the situation, that is, the external environment, which Freud refers to as alloplastic adaptation. In introducing the structural theory Freud did, however, not dispense with his original libido theory: by way of remodelling the reality in the case of psychosis the id nevertheless – albeit in a different way than in neurosis – can be said to assert its instinctual claims. This transforming of reality is that aspect of psychotic production, which is often found to be so very fascinating, since psychotic thinking does not only negate reality, but rather endeavours to create a new one. In that sense psychotic thinking bears a certain resemblance with utopian thinking, which also does not accept the factual conditions, but rather seeks to transform and rebuild them from scratch.

Hence, it can be said that by way of remodelling reality psychotic thinking manages to obey the demands of the instinctual impulses originating in the id: reality is thus transformed and reconstructed according to the principle of wish fulfilment. This is most evident in cases of megalomania where omnipotent phantasies regarding one's own self, prevail. But in cases of paranoia there also is evidence that there are similar mechanism at work that allow for the fulfilment of the instinctual wishes originating from the id: incidentally, this is in line with Claus Conrad's notion of *anastrophe* (described in Chapter 1 of the current book), a condition in which the patient feels, on the one hand, omnipotent but, on the other, he feels threatened and menaced, because everything revolves about himself. Although reality has now become threatening, this form of reality construction nonetheless allows the individual to feel important, not to be overlooked and to have meaning in the world.

Although it has to be admitted that Freud's structural theory of the id, the ego and the superego introduced a number of new theoretical aspects and thus contributed to a better understanding of psychosis, we have to nevertheless ask ourselves, if this theory does not actually represent a simplification and reduction of complexity compared with Freud's earlier theoretical accounts with respect to psychotic experience. After all, several crucial questions are left open: What do we now make of the difference between word-presentation and thing-presentation? And what do we make of the difference between the retreat into one's own ego and the return to the object? The structural theory does not take into consideration these two questions that, nevertheless, continue to be of utmost importance for the understanding of psychosis.

Pathological narcissism and relationship formation (after Freud)

Psychogenesis and biogenesis are not incompatible opposites

The vulnerability–stress–coping model attempts to frame psychotic and affective disorders based on a biopsychosocial perspective. According to this model the pathogenesis of schizophrenic disorder is considered a combination of vulnerability, which can be congenital, early formative and stressful experiences, and the subject's own personal coping mechanisms. Even if nowadays it is generally accepted that both biology and psychology should not be seen as opposites (i.e. that they both play a decisive role in the aetiology of the mental disorder, as well as in symptom formation and symptom development), the pertinent question still

36 Psychoanalytic theories about psychosis

remains: how to deal with the fact that biology and psychology are inter-dependent and must, therefore, not be played off against each other? In that respect Victor Tausk was one of the pioneers in that he endeavoured to understand psychosis along psychoanalytic principles.

Victor Tausk, who was one of Freud's most talented and creative early disciples, was constantly seeking to apply Freud's ideas and concepts to the understanding of the psychoses. During one of Tausk's lectures at a Wednesday meeting of the Psychoanalytic Society in Vienna, Freud incidentally became, on account of the closeness of Tausk's ideas to his own, more and more restless and eventually passed a note to Lou Andreas-Salomé with the words: 'Does he know *all* about it already?' The story of Tausk's conflictual relationship with Freud was to become after Tausk's savage suicide a cause for much speculation in respect to his person as well as the psychoanalytic movement in general. The particular circumstances of Tausk's death were especially cruel: he had fastened to a nail in his room a cord which he twisted into a noose, put his head in it and then fired a bullet from a pistol through his right temple. Paul Roazen (1973) clearly implied that Freud was ultimately responsible for Tausk's untimely death in 1919. Roazen is of the opinion that Tausk had many innovative ideas and independent thoughts, but that Freud would always put his own mark on anything Tausk succeeded in coming up with, which – at least according to Roazen – is the main explanation for Tausk's suicide. Two years after Roazen's publication, Kurt R. Eissler (1971), in his book *Talent and Genius*, raises substantial objections against these accusations put forward by Roazen. Eissler, too, considers Tausk as one of the most talented pychoanalysts of his time, who like Freud made many interesting contributions to psychiatry, especially with his clinical studies of the psychoses. But then Eissler reiterates his belief that in the end it turned out that only Freud had the ability to develop a viable methodological framework based on his numerous clinical observations, which proved Freud to be a true genius as distinct from those who are merely talented.

All the same, Tausk was indisputably one of the pioneers of his time to challenge the in those days commonly accepted scientific theoretical viewpoint that organicity and psychodynamics are incompatible. He refused to accept a scientific approach according to which a disease that can be organically explained, cannot be also investigated and understood along psychoanalytic principles. And that's why in a psychoanalytic paper from 1915 he put forward his ideas and clinical observations on 'the psychology of the alcoholic occupation delirium'. There he writes:

> The occupation delirium (of the alcoholic) can thus only be a coitus-wish delirium. This, like a dream, represents the fulfilment of a wish the sufferer is not fully capable of fulfilling in his normal waking life and is totally incapable of fulfilling in the state of toxicosis. He took to alcohol, after all, because the other sex had left him dissatisfied. His dearest wish would have been to achieve a satisfactory love relationship with the other sex. Now he drinks and

Psychoanalytic theories about psychosis 37

alcohol liberates his libido, but at the same time it makes him impotent. . . . This [delirium] gives him a sense of competence and self-assurance, the 'this-I-am-good-at' feeling experienced by the patient whose occupation dream we analyzed. Both in the delirium and in the dream, 'working' is equivalent to engaging in coitus.

(Tausk 1914b: 114)

Even if we have to admit that these formulations, written at a time long since passed, may sound somewhat antiquated or alien to our ears today, and even if we do not perfectly agree with all of Tausk's interpretations, he nevertheless deserves special praise that he very early on adopted a firm position and openly articulated his view that there is no justifiable reason of not making use of psychoanalytic concepts and psychodynamic principles in order to study psychiatric syndromes, even if the organic causes are irrefutably proven. In any case, it is worth noting that Tausk was ahead of other significant authorities in the field of psychiatry in that he very early on challenged and debated the by then common and established scientific theoretical view of the irreconcilability of organicity and psychogeneity:

The fact that functional disturbance can be caused either by a known or an unknown toxin on the one hand or by a psychological impediment on the other is no reason why we should refrain from inquiring into the psychological mechanism of the disturbance and its specifically psychological background. This must be mostly explicitly stated, in view of the circumstance that certain clinicians wish to bar psychoanalysis from the exploration of mental disturbances for which an organic etiology has been established.

(Tausk 1914b: 96)

Sadly, this scientific-theoretical approach could not become broadly established in the field of mental health. Otherwise all of these many years of unfruitful controversies and debates concerning the issue of psychogenic or somatogenic origin of psychotic conditions would have been quite unnecessary. Even to this day it is by far no common practice to examine the biological mechanisms of psychiatric disorders and to also try to consider them alongside with and in relation to psychodynamic factors. Both sides, psychodynamically oriented psychotherapists as well as psychiatrists, who favour a biologically oriented approach, should for the benefit of their patients finally consent to abide to certain professional ethical principles in this controversial discussion, as for instance: to not ignore and be principally open to the various scientific research findings in the field of neurosciences, genetics and pharmacology.

The psychotic and the body

However, what Tausk became truly famous for is his paper 'On the Origin of the "Influencing Machine" in Schizophrenia'. Since its publication in 1919, this work has never ceased to inspire subsequent authors, who probably were first of all struck by its intriguing title, so much so that the term came to be used in all sorts of contexts, where occasionally the term had nothing to do anymore with the original diagnosis, or the original idea behind the concept. Tausk, who had made great efforts to further develop the concept of projection in a clinical psychiatric context, eventually came up with the idea of the 'influencing machine': on the basis of clinical observations of his adult patients he reached the conclusion that the common schizophrenic delusion of being influenced by machines in a persecutory way has to be conceived of as an externalised projection of the patient's own body. And so what Tausk suggests is that sometimes it is not another person, but an anonymous apparatus, a machine-like thing or a technical device, which becomes the patient's target of projections of persecutory anxieties. But if this is the case, on what basis can this be explained and interpreted? In answering this question Tausk first follows Freud, who had postulated that delusional psychosis involved a regression of libido back to primary narcissism, whereby the most primitive stage of child development invariably involves the child's concentration on his own body. In the attempt to show how schizophrenic symptoms can represent the earliest stages of the ego's contact with reality, Tausk then asks himself, what it is exactly that gets projected, when the danger is experienced by the psychotic patient as coming from an 'influencing machine'. Tausk comes to the following conclusion:

> The evolution by distortion of the human apparatus into a machine is a projection that corresponds to the development of the pathological process which converts the ego into a diffuse sexual being, or – expressed in the language of the genital period – into a genital, a machine independent of the aims of the ego and subordinated to a foreign will.
>
> (Tausk 1914a: 213)

It seems worthwhile to have a closer look at this approach which, at first glance, may appear rather difficult to understand. First of all, we might want to find out what the essence of Tausk's ideas, formulated in the currently no longer used language of drive psychology, is and what they have to say to us still today. After we have subjected the above quotation to closer scrutiny, it seems to allow the following conclusions: The influencing machine is the production of a progressive, chronic psychosis. And this involves a process in which the psychotic patient transforms his body into something alien and inanimate and in a further stage into the 'influencing machine'. All this entails a massive alienation of sexuality that becomes increasingly detached from the ego, and is subsequently leading a life of its own: The entire (body) ego is being suffused with sexuality which implies the regression of libido to an early infantile stage and which determines the retransformation of the genitally centralised libido into the pregenital stage, 'in which the entire body is a libidinal zone – in which the entire body is a genital' (ibid.: 212). This is a result of the delibidinisation of the external world. The libido

Psychoanalytic theories about psychosis 39

is withdrawn from the objects and stored in an undifferentiated form in the inside of the body in the wake of which the narcissistic libidinal cathexis of the body gains ascendancy which brings with it an (uncanny) awareness of body functions, that is, an invasion into consciousness of something which normally remains unconscious or preconscious. The whole body now being libidinally over-cathected and suffused with primitive aggression is in danger of exploding and disintegrating into fragments, a situation which leads to bodily sensations and experiences that remain unintegrated and unsynthesised, and thus appearing to come from, or impinge from, the outside and are therefore attributed not to the activity of one's own body, but to the activity of alien powers or demons and take on a definitely 'uncanny' and menacing quality. And so it can be said that the influencing machine is a projection of the patient's unintegrated and disconnected bodily sensations in his desperate attempt at fending off massive persecutory anxieties he has no other means of coping with.

At the beginning of the schizophrenic psychosis there are the patient's perceived bodily changes: at first the patient still experiences himself as the originator of these changes but as the delusion progresses these bodily sensations are projected on to the outside world and thus are experienced as alien influences coming from a source outside of the patient's body. And now the ego has lost its capacity to develop on the basis of the identification with the unified and stable image of the body – a thesis put forward by Jacques Lacan a few decades later. Throughout life the ego develops on the basis of the narcissistic cathexis of the body image, in order to protect itself against the inner stimuli of bodily functions or genital excitations, otherwise experienced as uncontrollable and 'persecutory'.

It was the child psychoanalyst Paula Elkisch (1959), who many years later in her clinical investigations of the work with psychotic children has built upon Tausk's paper on the influencing machine. She postulates a breakdown of the perceptual integrative capacity of the ego which is responsible for the serious impediment of ego development and the subsequent onset of psychotic experiences. When, however, defence mechanisms such as denial can no longer cope with the endogenous stimuli which are continually generated by physiological processes in the organism itself and which are very close to the instinctual drives not neutralised by the body, there is no escape anymore from the enteroceptive and proprioceptive excitations that gain prominence and force themselves continually into the sensorium and which now assume a predominantly aggressive character. In order to get rid of these delibidinised and quasi-animated forces they have to be projected on to the external objects, whereby these objects are then vested with the child's internal psychotic reality which is experienced as if his body were powered by ego-alien demonical forces with the result that these external objects then become extremely uncanny, aggressive and persecutory assuming a mechanical quality just as is the child's own body image.

It would appear, though, that it is not strictly necessary to follow trail of the entire intertwining flow and wealth of ideas put forward by Tausk, in order to be able to appreciate Tausk's ingenuity of conception in his classical paper on the

40 Psychoanalytic theories about psychosis

'influencing machine' that won Tausk a pioneering place in the psychological understanding of schizophrenic delusions, and where he turns the spotlight particularly on the special significance of bodily perception in delusional experience. Clinically such patients present with an undue amount of awareness for the body as a whole, or for parts of the body, which pierces the patient's consciousness and occupies his thoughts.

The narcissistic cathexis of the body serves as a protective function to the psychotic patient's fragmented self. Once the experience of a unified self is no longer guaranteed and thoughts are no longer experienced as one's own thoughts, then the perception of one's own body may be the last resort to afford the psychotic patient a sense of a coherent and narrowly stable self. If we infer that the constitution of the self is originally based on the image of an apparently unified body, then the retreat into one's own body has to be considered a regression – a reassurance of one's own identity with the aid of heightened body awareness. This is a mechanism we frequently encounter in cases of severe (borderline) personality disorders with self-harming behaviour. This self-harming behaviour represents a dynamic which is likely to pursue the same goal: to feel the painful sensation on the surface of the body, that is, on the skin, since this affords the patient to feel and experience the boundaries of his own body and the boundaries of his own self.

The quality of psychotic object relationships

Now, let's get back to the better known and more influential disciples of Freud. Melanie Klein (1946) made herself known for her outstanding theoretical contributions in regard to the understanding of the origins and vicissitudes of the aggressive or destructive tendencies. Klein's work initiated a revolutionary change of the way of thinking in psychoanalysis, particularly in view of the psychotic processes that from now on were no longer merely considered as being characteristic of the insane person, whereas the neurotic mode of functioning was seen as typical for the 'normal' person. What Klein basically would imply is that psychotic thinking is not so foreign to all of us. She found that Freud's concept of stages of development through which the child passes in well-defined order was too limiting. Her idea of 'positions' differed from Freud's 'stages' in that Klein did not think we ever grow out of them. Klein describes two positions – the paranoid-schizoid position and the depressive position – as different ways of dealing with anxiety. And she felt that there was a continuous tension between paranoid-schizoid and depressive mechanisms throughout life, whereby people constantly move from one position to the other and back again. And thus we can see that it finds itself already reflected in the choice of Kleinian terminology what her key concern is: Throughout life the paranoid mechanisms and phantasies are available and are likely to be used when under any kind of mental stress or strain.

In the paranoid-schizoid position part-object relationships prevail in the infant's early unconscious phantasy life. Persecutory anxiety is met by processes that threaten to fragment the mind. Processes of splitting the object into bad and good

Psychoanalytic theories about psychosis 41

are characteristic. Because in the earliest period of life destructive tendencies are predominant, it is important to distinguish between bad and good objects and thus keep the good objects alive. At the early period of life the integration of life instincts and death instincts is not yet possible. Part-object relationships are predominant: the good or the bad breast, the powerful or destructive penis. Envy is held to be innate in origin as part of the instinctual endowment: it is a destructive attack on the sources of life, – in Kleinian language – on the good and feeding breast. Spoiling the breast and robbing it of its contents are characteristic features of envy. This has serious consequences: as a result of the envious forcing of the self into the object to occupy it and spoil it, the introjection and identification with a stable good object is prevented.

With the outbreak of a psychotic illness these early infantile phantasies may once again take centre stage. The concrete thinking, typical for the schizophrenic delusion, is based on the undifferentiation of psychic and bodily experience, and in that sense can be seen as a regression to the early infantile state of undifferentiatedness. In the mind of the subject penis and breast become the all-powerful and persecutory objects they once were: the breast that feeds and guarantees survival, and the penis that is all-powerful and creates life.

> Mrs F. complains about sensing something hard and cold inside of her. More precisely, she cannot escape the feeling that there is a piece of iron rod stuck in her body. And, at the same time, she can hear the voice of her step-sister, who reproaches and upbraids her over and over again. Mrs F. suffers from strong feelings of guilt; and she has the urge to punish herself for something that has to do with the iron rod inside of her. Yet, by the same token, she cannot really explain what these reproaches are about or why she should feel guilty. What's more, she is persuaded that her neighbours persecute her and that they maintain constant watch over her house and over every move she makes through video surveillance and laser light.
>
> Mrs F. is an attractive woman and although highly delusional she has not lost relation to reality altogether and obviously maintains some contact to the outside world. She tries to get a grip on herself and hides her feelings, because more than anything else she is afraid of being labelled as completely mad and insane.

Her husband takes care of her in a sympathetic and realistic way. That is, he neither seems to deny the fact that his wife suffers from a mental illness, nor does he stop loving her. They both suffer from the fact that they have no children. The reliable base of support due to her husband's proximity, without him ever becoming overprotective or overanxious, gives Mrs F. all the more strength to keep on going. And this is quite in opposition to how it was in the past and still is with her family of origin. She still lives in the same village as her family of origin, and even lives in the same building complex. From an early age onwards her parents restricted her independence and autonomy. They never ever gave her the freedom

42 Psychoanalytic theories about psychosis

to make up her own mind and to take a decision on her own authority. This situation has not changed much until today. Presumably due to her beauty and attractive appearance, she was considered to be seductive and also open to abuse. It gradually becomes apparent that there is some kind of taboo surrounding the members of the patient's family of origin, which means that the question remains unanswered as to whether or not the father has sexually abused his own daughter.

What lies in this particular case at the core of the psychotic experience is the intrusive object which is stuck in the patient's body: an iron rod inside the vagina, which is the source of pain that never ceases or subsides. Most likely, in this case it is a sexualised object: what makes it so dangerous for the patient – there is recurrently a high risk of suicidality – is that she is thoroughly convinced that she is to be held responsible for it (the object) being stuck inside her. It is not clear, though, what it is she blames or punishes herself for. From what she says it seems more likely that she feels guilty for early excessive masturbatory activities than that there had actually been exposure to an early sexual trauma. The persecutory object apparently is a concretisation of her thoughts and feelings: the object, possibly a penis, which could have taken possession of her and which is now stuck inside her vagina, is transformed into an iron rod, that is, a never tiring and inexhaustible force that fills up and stimulates her vagina such that she is in constant pain. This bad phallic object is seemingly not related to anything, not to any person and not to any history. It seems that there is no relativisation or regulation in regard to the absolute and invasive destructiveness of the object and, consequently, there is also no reduction of guilt and anxiety.

The transition from the paranoid-schizoid position into the depressive position may be experienced as threatening and always represents some kind of crisis. The associated feelings are characteristically ambivalent. If there is a failure to reach and preserve the depressive position this may be experienced as a depressive breakdown instead of a newly achieved capacity to mourn and to repair and be constructive despite the destructive impulses inside. This state of affairs may be met with manic defences as a way of dealing with fear and to perhaps resort to omnipotence as a destructive controlling force, as it is characteristic for the paranoid-schizoid position.

> Mrs C. describes herself as an autodidact. She says that she acquired the educational canon all by herself through private study. She wants to speak with her individual therapist about extremely tricky issues, such as Spinoza's ethics, Schopenhauer's relation to women and things alike. What finally caused her breakdown was the separation from her husband. After an affair ten years ago he recently had cheated on his wife once again. Mrs C. has brought up four children. After her marriage she had no longer her own career in mind, but focussed on the success of her husband and now she had to learn that he has a lover. At present she feels totally helpless and in her despair she wants to just end her life. When her therapist interprets her talking about everything and anything as an attempt to divert attention or flee from her own

problem, Mrs C. reacts with incomprehension or rather with utmost indignation. In that particular therapy session she appears entirely distraught and finally says that everything that was important to her has now been taken away from her, so that therefore she now feels completely at a loss. How can this be understood? As a result of the therapist's explicitly addressing the issue of the crisis, which the patient is currently experiencing, Mrs C. now, all of a sudden, feels utterly deprived of her manic defence.

With the achievement of the depressive position comes the capacity to experience the object as a whole object. This implies a new attitude, a new relation to the object, where the object can now be seen more realistically, with different characteristics and different qualities. With the term 'reparation' Klein describes an important impulse and a crucial outcome of the depressive position. The pain of guilt, loss and concern is turned into constructive effort of an altruistic kind, because the depressive position brings with it the capacity to recognise the attack and damage previously done to the object in the paranoid-schizoid position and the subsequent wish to make good that previous damage and repair the object. This is also the moment of remorse when the object can be experienced as independent and not only as persecutory and when feelings of love and the recognition that the object is also good, has concern and is caring, arise and now supersede the persecutory anxieties and the feelings of aggression. Envy fades into the background and gratitude towards the object is brought out.

The analysis of strong and weak points of the various contributions to the development of psychoanalytic theory after Freud can probably best be achieved by comparing the different conceptions of the relationship to the object, in other words, the subject's relationship to the other. While it is true that the real challenge and the value of Klein's theory lies in the fact that she has placed even greater emphasis on the object relationships, whereby she was particularly interested in mental contents, that is, in the phantasies and imaginations of the infant conceived of – more or less – as an independent entity whose knowledge of the object depends on the degree of integration of the instinctual drives and wishes aimed at the object, Klein left relatively unexplored the role of the environment. Again, Klein enriched psychoanalytic theory enormously in that she delineated the complex nature of very early mental activity (i.e. of phantasies and mental pictures) in relation to the object (the significant other), and she also proposed a sequence of these mental pictures depending on the developmental phases or degree of integration of the instincts; and this has also proven to be of particular relevance in the treatment of patients who suffer from psychoses. So, despite the fact that Klein in her thinking paid little attention to the interpersonal aspect, but remained focussed upon the subject's internal phantasy world and thus – one can say – undervalued the role of the real other (i.e. the influence of the external object upon the subject), it nevertheless is true that Wilfred R. Bion, for instance, could utilise Klein's theories (above all her concept of projective identification) as the basis for developing a conception that bridges the intrapsychic and the interpersonal.

44 Psychoanalytic theories about psychosis

At around the same time as Bion has developed his conception of the container/contained, Donald W. Winnicott has developed equally relevant conceptions, such as for instance, his concept of the potential space, etc. – and it cannot be emphasised enough just how the contributions of both these two prominent psychoanalytic thinkers have been highly beneficial for psychoanalysis to the present day.

Autism and psychosis

Eugen Bleuler was a Swiss psychiatrist and most notable for his contributions to the understanding of mental illness and for coining not only the term 'schizophrenia', but also the term 'autism'. According to Bleuler, autism is the paramount feature in schizophrenia, where the schizophrenic patient seems to exhibit progressive loss of contact with reality and thus retreats into his own self. But the shutting-off of relations between the self and the outside world is to be considered not merely as a deficit, but also as an attempt at protecting one's own self and keeping the pieces of the broken self together. In the attempt to capture this autistic layer of experiencing from a developmental-psychological perspective Thomas H. Ogden (1992), the distinguished and internationally renowned psychoanalyst, who has since long been in a critical and creative dialogue with the Kleinian school of thought, has proposed the idea of an 'autistic-contiguous' position as a way of conceptualising a psychological organisation which is more primitive than either the paranoid-schizoid or the depressive position proposed by Melanie Klein. In his clinical and theoretical investigations Ogden has described the autistic-contiguous mode as a sensory dominated, pre-symbolic mode of generating experience. In this autistic-contiguous mode it is primarily experiences of sensations, particularly at the skin surface, that are the principal media for the creation of psychological meaning where sensory contiguity of skin surface, along with the element of rhythmicity, are basic to the organisation of a rudimentary sense of self and object and thus can be also viewed as a precursor to symbol formation. Once again we can see that it is the bodily sensations and bodily perceptions that play a vital role.

The clinical relevance of the autistic-contiguous mode of experiencing may best be illustrated by way of a clinical example.

> Mr S. is a good-looking man, but he also looks a little scruffy. He receives part-time inpatient psychotherapeutic treatment. He does not talk about what he really expects from therapy, but rather indulges in overly formal, cliché-ridden statements: He has lost his job because he repeatedly got into an argument with his former chef. Besides, he would like to come off the alcohol and the cannabis. What he says has invariably the quality of a throwaway remark, his words seem to be to no effect and, as a corollary of that, they do not find an open and receptive ear. His words seem to bear no relation to his inner reality. It takes only a few days to make him an outsider, who is neither liked by his fellow patients nor by the female therapists in the clinic. His individual therapist feels troubled and distressed by Mr S, since when he talks to her he

seems to be unable to keep the appropriate distance, so that she is invariably given the feeling of being intruded upon.

What he says is too confusing and contradictory to establish any emotional rapport to him. Only listening to the manner, in which he speaks, allows the therapist to finally bridge the gap and to reach some kind of understanding. There is his constant chatter leaving hardly a moment of silence and his mostly talking in stereotypes. What's more, he seems to be completely unaware of the fact that what he says is frequently quite offensive to the other person and that he also sounds rather arrogant – but it is, at the same time, obvious that it is not his intention to be destructive. It is rather as though he is intent on wrapping himself in words, like in a cloak or 'second skin'. It now has become clear that his words are not used for communication but rather for self-soothing purposes, that is, for creating a protective enveloping cocoon around himself, some kind of boundary between inner and outer space.

Esther Bick (1987) proposed a type of defence which she referred to as 'second skin formation'. This is according to Bick a self-protective effort at resurrecting a feeling of integrity of one's own surface as a defensive reaction to a disturbance of the 'primal skin function'. Bick describes occasions, in which this achievement of the primal skin's container function goes totally wrong, with the result that the personality simply leaks uncontainedly out into a limitless space, because of being devoid of any capacity to contain the parts of the self. The concept of 'second skin' may help to better understand why in the presence of Mr S. the other person is inevitably given the feeling that there is something strange and peculiar about him. First of all, there is to be mentioned his profuse sweating which could almost be described as something like a haze dome of smell, in which he wraps himself up and which can be perceived as extremely unpleasant by the other person. And then, there is also his habit of sitting down at the piano and tapping with his two index fingers unremittingly on the key board, mechanically playing the same melody over and over again: This seems to be an autistic activity, which can tyrannise all the others around him, but which affords the patient to form a sound envelope, an acoustic second skin, or else, as in the case of sweating, an olfactory second skin. I shall now return to the clinical example to provide a further sense of what I am trying to discuss:

> In order to better understand the predicament and desperation of Mr S., we have to first of all focus our attention on the early infantile life with typically sensation-dominated forms of experiences that serve the function that the infant in relation to and contact with his significant others – which includes being touched, held, nursed and attended to in various other ways – is granted the opportunity to achieve the earliest sense of boundedness, the sense of having a surface and a place, where his own experience occurs and where a sense of structure, order and containment is generated; in other words, what's granted is the opportunity to develop a – albeit rudimentary and primitive –

46 Psychoanalytic theories about psychosis

sense of 'self'. But because Mr S. in his early life was deprived of being touched and responded to by the primary attachment figure on the basis of which he could have constituted his earliest 'self' experience, he now in his adult life has to utilise, for self-soothing purposes, the surface of the other as an autistic substitute for an incompletely developed or deteriorating sense of his own surface. But, of course, this literally clinging to the other person is unavoidably bound to be the source of many misunderstandings, since the other person cannot know that all these clinging forms of sensory connectedness to an object are experienced by Mr S., momentarily at least, as holding the parts of his sensory-dominated personality together. And thus the sole effect of his way of being and behaving is to only push the other people even further away.

Why does Mr S., all the same, insist on being a highly sensitive person, much to the surprise of his interlocutors? By this he can't possibly mean to say that he is acting on the basis of empathy or intuition. It rather seems that the patient's efforts are to be viewed as an attempt to supply himself with a second skin by making use of the surface of the object as if it were his own. By sticking bits of the surface of the object to his own failing surface the patient attempts to defend against the anxiety of disintegration. Donald Meltzer (1975) has introduced the term 'adhesive identification' to refer to the defensive adherence to the object in the service of allaying the anxiety of disintegration. Francis Tustin (1972), who became known for her research findings of various forms of childhood autism which are predominantly psychogenic, preferred the term 'adhesive equation' to the term 'adhesive identification', because, in this defensive process, the individual's body is equated with the object in the most concrete, sensory way. All this makes it perhaps easier to now understand why Mr S. has to employ imitation and mimicry, or at times even violence, in an effort to make use of the other person's skin or surface. And this also explains why particularly the female interlocutors tend to experience Mr S. as offensive, invasive or even violent, and thus try to keep out of his way. But if there is, nevertheless, at times some contact or encounter with Mr S., he will be experienced by his conversation partners as being rude or even as sexually abusive, notably if the interlocutor is a woman.

> Because Mr S.'s mode of relating to others has to be considered as basically being in the service of self-soothing, self-limitation and self-touching, and because – as the case material clearly evidences – it cuts off relations with real external objects, it has to be understood as an autistic mode of defence, in which this autistic activity is a substitute formation utilised to provide the patient with the illusion of experiencing himself, whereas in reality the patient experiences despair and alienation, which is connected with the feeling of not being able to ever achieve any kind of self-knowledge or self-experience on the basis of truly getting in 'touch' with the other.

Thus, in the 'autistic-contiguous mode' psychic organisation is established through the body's capacity to experience sensory contiguity (i.e. sensory surfaces touching one another). The case example demonstrates, how certain forms of self-soothing behaviour are rather to be seen as an autistic activity of self-touching and as such are a 'surrogate' or substitute for genuine inter-subjective contact.

Learning from experience in the psychotic process

People who develop a psychotic illness later on in life, contain in their psyche a non-psychotic part of the personality, although they simultaneously contain also a psychotic part, which is often so dominant that the non-psychotic part of the personality is almost obscured by it. Wilfred R. Bion disagreed with Melanie Klein, who held the view that schizophrenic mechanisms arise out of an excessive use of normal projective processes in the paranoid-schizoid position. He evolved a theory of his own to explain how the psychic apparatus becomes schizophrenic: Bion postulates that those people who would later in life develop a schizophrenic illness negotiated the paranoid-schizoid position in a qualitatively different way from other people, due to a fragmentation of the psyche, resulting in the formation of a psychotic part of the personality which thus is left functioning essentially different from the non-psychotic part of the personality that is split off from the psychotic part, a process which is, according to Bion, active from very early on in life.

So what are the preconditions for the mechanisms on which the psychotic part of the personality develops? There are four essential features for a person to be prone to psychosis (Bion 1957):

- A strong preponderance of destructive impulses.
- These impulses lead to an intolerable hatred of internal and external realities.
- This hatred results in a dread of imminent annihilation – which in turn leads to a premature and precipitate formation of object relations.
- The fourth feature is thus the formation of object relationships which are premature, precipitate, and intensely dependent.

Due to hatred of internal and external realities, the infant makes attacks on his own perceptual apparatus with the result that psychic links are destroyed or prevented from emerging. There may be various reasons for that, which can be found in the very early object-relationships: the breakdown of the emotional link between mother/father and infant; the incapacity or unwillingness of the significant others to attune and adapt to the infant's needs; or the invasiveness of the object. If the emotional links are cut off, the result is a 'minute splitting': the infant splits his objects and, simultaneously, parts of his own self, that is, all that which would make him aware of the reality he so much hates, into exceedingly minute fragments. But instead of merely splitting off and projecting multifaceted mental pictures or integral self- and object-representations the schizophrenic individual, by contrast,

48 Psychoanalytic theories about psychosis

is fragmenting perceptual functions, mostly closely connected with bodily sensations, into isolated component parts and then projects these functions into the object, which is, as a result of this, experienced as uncanny, as having a life of its own and, because it is not really separated from the self, is experienced as an entrapment. And this is what Bion termed a 'bizarre object'. For instance, the perception of some intolerable internal voice or sound, or possibly a single word, is projected by the schizophrenic into a gramophone, or rather into the patient's representation of a gramophone, and thus becomes a 'bizarre object' felt to be capable of spying on and talking to the patient. The patient's own hateful attacks are now felt to come from the outside (i.e. from the object), felt to have a completely autonomous existence outside himself and to persecute him. This means, the patient's hostility has been projected and installed into the object.

What makes the 'minute splitting' such a tricky and extremely challenging thing is that it renders reintegration or 'containment' almost impossible. Along with it, the thinking capacity is severely impaired, since that part of the perceptual or psychic apparatus, required for thinking, has now been expelled and projected into the 'bizarre objects'. The psychotic part of the personality is characterised by fragmenting and evacuative processes and is therefore not equipped with the function to produce any thinking activity. In this context Bion explains the significant function of the 'ideographs', which he considers as visual precursors of thinking. When the parts that were projected into the bizarre objects return, this is invariably experienced as an attack of the previously expelled objects. And thus the psychotic defence organisation predominantly engages in an activity of evacuation and getting rid of unbearable inner states, and not of processing or digesting them. If the capacity to tolerate frustration is poorly developed and thus massive projective identification is increasingly employed in order to get rid of bad or intolerable experiences, this may lead to a situation, where the gap between the psychotic and the non-psychotic parts of the personality grows even wider, until the psychic apparatus is completely stripped off of any capacity to represent or symbolise.

Wilfred R. Bion constructed a 'theory of thinking', in which he described how the sane or non-psychotic part of the personality develops. Now, the question has to be asked: How can an apparatus for thinking develop (or perhaps re-develop), capable to learn from experience, or in other words, to deal with the various, often unexpected happenings in one's life and psychically process and digest them? According to Bion, psychic or mental processing involves three steps:

1   At the beginning, there is a pre-existing thought, a 'preconception', which is not yet an idea or a conception, but is only the potential for a conception.
2   It becomes an idea or conception when it meets its realisation (i.e. when there is an emotional experience of satisfaction). However, in case of satisfaction, representational form cannot be given to this experience. Only if a preconception links with a frustration that can be tolerated, in other words, if a preconception meets with a negative realisation, can experience be given representational form.

Psychoanalytic theories about psychosis 49

3 But in this context we cannot afford to leave unmentioned that only if this frustration, this linking of preconceptions and negative realisations, takes place in a loving atmosphere which is protected by a significant other, will this then engender a process which leads to 'learning from experience'.

The reason why this repeated interaction with the other is such an essential requirement is that it helps the infant to discriminate new experience from that which had been anticipated. In other words, it allows the infant – if all goes well – to learn from experience (i.e. to first become aware of, to realise and eventually make use of the difference between the actual and the anticipated object, between external and internal, between self and object), which then in due time will allow for claiming phantasy for oneself by way of differentiating phantasy from reality and thus constitute *phantasy as such*. All this is needed to acquire a function which Bion termed the alpha function: 'The activity that I have here described by two individuals becomes introjected by the infant so that the container-contained apparatus becomes installed in the infant as part of the apparatus of alpha-function' (Bion 1962: 91).

It must be borne in mind that what is internalised is the interaction (and not a specific quality of the object), which prepares the ground for the acquisition of the alpha function. It is the object's 'containing-function' and meaning-generating, more mature mental apparatus that processes and detoxifies the evoked feelings, which thus makes available for reinternalisation of a more manageable and integrable version of that which had previously been projected.

The containing or reverie function is instrumental in constituting the alpha function, which transforms sense impressions, i.e. raw sensory data or beta elements, into alpha elements, which cohere as they proliferate in order to form the contact barrier. This contact barrier is according to Bion continuously in process of formation and marks the point of contact and separation between conscious and unconscious elements and originates the distinction between them and thus makes it possible to process and digest emotional experience. It is important to note that under the aegis of the alpha function projective identification does not only stay in the service of unburdening the psyche of overwhelming tension and unbearable feelings, but is transformed into an empathic exchange, a true interpersonal communication. So one can conclude that unless there has been granted the opportunity to develop an alpha function of one's own, there can be neither learning from experience nor psychic or mental development, to the detrimental effect that beta elements can only be evacuated and expelled, but not transformed, psychically bound or integrated or intrapsychically repressed.

This account gives us an idea of what's required when therapeutically working with psychotic patients: the therapist has to be prepared to make himself emotionally available to the patient's psychotic experience and fulfil the essential function of a containing and metabolising object. Theoretically this seems not to pose too great a problem, since Bion's model allows a clear and systematic assessment. But clinically the challenges are enormous and working with psychotic patients can

50 Psychoanalytic theories about psychosis

put a huge strain on the therapeutic relationship, because to endure and contain the patient's 'minute splitting' and his projections of unintegrated 'bizarre objects' will always be a difficult task for the therapist.

Foreclosure and the symbolic order

What's noteworthy and surprising is that the clinical concepts of the Lacanian school are rather pessimistic as far as the successful outcome of psychotherapeutic treatment of schizophrenic patients is concerned. Let me just quote one statement of a Lacanian follower, Thomas Vogt: 'What benefit can there be from psychotherapy for such cases? We would like to underscore that we are principally in accordance with Lacan's view that the psychotic structure basically cannot be altered by psychotherapeutic intervention' (Vogt 2007: 202).

This pessimistic assessment is an inevitable conclusion from Lacan's theory of the psychoses (for a critique of this therapeutic pessimism cf. Küchenhoff and Warsitz 1993). If there is failure of primal repression and of the formation of the symbolic structure, this leaves, according to Lacan, a hole in the symbolic order of the child that cannot be filled. This entails an absolute limitation of the thinking capacity, not only with regard to conscious processes in cognition but also with regard to the significant relationship of unconscious and conscious phantasies. And it is this, which accounts for the difference of repression from the defence mechanism of 'foreclosure', as it was described by Lacan.

Jacques Lacan draws upon Freud's short article on 'Fetishism' (Freud 1927) in which Freud describes how the ego rejects an incompatible idea together with an affect and behaves as if the idea has never occurred to the ego at all; the idea in this case is that there are two different sexes; or put differently, what is rejected is the fact that the mother lacks a penis. This reality is repudiated, as Freud says, and the fetish is then taken as a substitute for the mother's penis. The fetish serves the function of holding on to the unconscious idea that there is only one sex. What is thus repudiated or foreclosed, as Lacan says, is the presumed lack and, with it, the fact of the mutual dependency of the two sexes.

This is Lacan's point of departure. But it is important to keep in mind that Lacan's notion of foreclosure does not refer to the rejection of a conflictual desire, but it refers to something even more primitive and primordial (i.e. to a stage where the inner world of representations is still in the process of formation). If this process leaves one (or even several) 'holes' in the symbolic order, the result is that experiences cannot be 'metabolised' or, in other words: What's experienced cannot be relativised. And so it must be stressed that the recognition of the lack is not only essential for the recognition and acceptance of the difference of the two sexes, but also and especially for the successful development of the symbolic order. The symbolic order is based on a fundamental difference, as previously outlined in the chapter on the issue of concrete thinking. The symbol represents the thing, but it is not the thing itself. Lacan brings the point home by stating: 'The symbol is the murder of the thing' (Lacan 2006: 104).

The symbolic order yields the possibility of freedom; and we can thus take distance from reality. And we can also take distance from the significant others: the symbolic function prevents the developing child from being engulfed by his mother and allows the child to emerge as a separate entity in his or her own right. This squints toward the positive side of it. The negative side of it is the interdiction of 'jouissance', as Lacan put it. The word is not the thing itself; the love relationship does not allow to be completely wrapped up and merged in the other. The symbolic order, or the Symbolic, constitutes the matrix through which the child experiences his relationship to the others and thus introduces difference and distance, even where they have to be painfully experienced and where it is a question of overcoming them. What remains outside of the realm of the Symbolic cannot be symbolically transformed and metabolised by means of thought processes and feelings. Experiences located beyond the symbolic order become too insistent and intrusive and thus assume the connotations of the Real. They convey the sense of coming from the outside, because in absence of the symbolic function they cannot be held inside. But if no meaningful and symbolic sense can be made of these experiences the individual in the attempt to fill the empty space stages a limitless imaginary world, in which the unrestricted proliferation of phantasies and images prevails, so that the individual progressively enters into the realm of the Imaginary, as Lacan termed it. So in the absence of the symbolic function psychotic hallucinations and delusions are the consequent result of the individual's endeavour to make sense of what he or she experiences.

Now, in what way does the lack of the symbolic function affect the constitution and shaping of relationships? In Lacanian terminology the relevant principles can be summed up as follows. The 'object a' (*objet petit a*) stands for the unattainable imaginary object of desire. Normally it is relativised through the symbolic order. Imagination and symbolic representation are weighed against each other, and brought into perspective with the Real, which is not merely and simply identical with reality, since it is never to have directly and unfiltered but only indirectly and filtered through words and images. If the symbolic order collapses the imaginary object (a) of desire takes the place of the Big Other (A) of the symbolic order. As a consequence of this the desired object fills the subject's entire field of vision. This means that the references, relationships and dependencies which constitute the world of the symbolic and which link the object with other objects and with different aspects of reality are cut off and eliminated. If the narcissistic object becomes, so to speak, the whole world then this represents – to all intents and purposes – a major barrier to the possibility of relativisation with regard to the self as well as to the object. What is staged instead is a limitless imaginary world of self- and object images, which may give rise to phantasies of megalomania and feelings of persecution since the objects now have become larger than life.

Lacan offers an interesting theoretical conception of psychotic mechanisms. What in Lacan's perspective becomes especially apparent are the triggering conditions that release the psychotic process. These conditions are always connected with threshold situations or with some kind of maturational step, such as the

52 Psychoanalytic theories about psychosis

professional promotion into a leading position, or becoming oneself a father or mother etc. These are altogether situations, which confront the individual with the demands of symbolic triangulation, at which point the vulnerability of the individual's symbolic universe becomes apparent and thus re-invokes the primordial signifiers, that is, the origin of representation, which Lacan relates to the 'name-of-the-father' (Lacan 1988: 259). Ideally it is the father, who provides a basic triangulation from the start in order to initiate by the 'name-of-the-father' a symbolic universe.

That Lacan's ideas are no longer in conformity with contemporary principles and conceptions of gender studies should not blind us to the fact that Lacan has drawn our attention to the key principle of paternity (i.e. the relation of the father to son as central to the child's psychic development), which has lost none of its relevance to this day. Lacan emphasises that the symbolic father is not the real father, that is, an actual subject, but a position in the symbolic order, and that's why Lacan proposed the concept of the 'name-of-the-father'. He thus barters for a conceptual shortcoming which brings with it many clinical disadvantages and which can only be made up for in the actual therapeutic work with the individual patient. Lacan, for example, does not describe what it is that in the early object relationships prevents the identification with the 'primordial father', as Freud called him.

But there is another, even more severe disadvantage, which necessitates a critical response: Lacan's psychoanalytic model of a structural defect in psychotic conditions such as schizophrenia has the disadvantage in that it has never been extended to a therapeutic regimen that overcomes a profoundly pessimistic approach. Such a pessimistic view may be due to the fact that Lacan hypothesises that the origins of the symbolic defects lie at such an early stage of life. So, in order to find an answer to the question of how the therapeutic processes could possibly have a positive effect on the psychotic patient's special vulnerability, the Lacanian theoretical approach has always been linked to or combined with clinical approaches that are committed to other theoretical models.

The limits of language and the limits of thought

The analysis of the weak points of the Lacanian approach confronts us with the question of whether Klein's and Bion's specific object relations theories might be suited to step in where Lacan's model proves insufficient in terms of clinical applicability (Heim 2005; Burgoyne and Sullivan 1997). The recognition of the need to establish a creative debate about the similarities and differences of the psychoanalytic ideas of the two major psychoanalytic thinkers Klein and Lacan is not new. And although there have already been some attempts to realising this project it has so far not been systematically approached. If we assume that in psychoanalysis theory and technique are closely related, then such a dialogue may be extremely helpful, particularly in view of the psychotherapeutic treatment of psychotic patients. If we decide to take Lacan's theory of psychosis as a starting point there

Psychoanalytic theories about psychosis 53

is a crucial question we have still failed to resolve: is it possible to go beyond the psychotic patient's resistance (i.e. beyond the foreclosure of the symbolic) through and in the therapeutic process? But if Lacan's assumption is correct that what is rejected in the symbolic, that is, what is not inscribed in the symbolic order returns from without or the 'real' (Lacan 1993: 46), then the relevant question with regard to the psychotherapy with psychotic patients would have to be: how to deal with these projections within the therapeutic setting? Or, asked differently: To what extent is the therapist capable of receiving and containing the psychotic patient's unbounded psychic experiences, that is, his forcefully emitted beta elements, and subsequently returning them to the patient in a transformed and more metabolised form?

It is probably no coincidence that normally psychoanalysts committed to the object relations theory, have a much more optimistic view as far as the treatment of psychoses is concerned (Volkan 1995; Hartwich and Gruber 2003). This may perhaps be due to the fact that Klein's and likewise Bion's concepts were developed out of the actual day-to-day encounter with the patients in the psychoanalytic work and therefore are particularly suited for providing a therapeutic space in which new and previously unthought-of possibilities may emerge and be explored. On the other hand this may bring with it the risk of unrealistic optimism to which the linguo-genetic approach of Lacan could be a counterpoise.

Now, let's look more closely at the similarities and the differences of either the Lacanian conceptualisation or that of Bion. In both, Lacan and Bion, there is an emphasis on the capacity for producing representations which provide access to experiences: Bion emphasises the development of the capacity of thinking, whereas in Lacan's account it is the primordial paternal function that is the symbolic pathway into the symbolic order which is essential. But both theories claim that in order to develop an inner world of phantasies and imaginations the infant has to first recognise and integrate experiences of lack, absence, negation and renunciation. The awareness of a need not satisfied is, according to Bion, a prerequisite of the formation of concepts. According to Lacan the symbolic order is constituted on the basis of a lack of being, that is, on the ultimately unbridgeable gap between subject and object or other.

The strength of Lacan's conceptualisation lies in the fact that it brought linguistic and structuralistic approaches to psychoanalysis. It is clear that by working with the structure of language, this allowed Lacan to grasp more precisely the loss of language and of speech in psychosis and furthermore it allowed him to conceive of the deficient function of language and of speech as lying at the core of the psychotic structure. In as far as the differences between these two thinkers are concerned, Bion, for his part, by making extensive and intensive use of his clinical observations was particularly interested in the role played by the significant others, such as the parents, but also the therapist. But exceeding beyond this he especially wanted to find out more about the creative possibilities and potentials arising from these relationships with the significant others, by means of which psychic representations and thoughts could be promoted. On the basis of his clinical

54 Psychoanalytic theories about psychosis

investigations he then developed a variety of relevant concepts, as for instance his concept of reverie, or his idea of detoxifying aggressive and toxic phantasies through emotional containment and the metabolising alpha function.

The vital importance of the recognition of difference – case example

The following case example, described in some detail, tries to demonstrate what a pivotal role language can play in the endeavour of psychotherapist and patient working towards an awareness and recognition of 'difference' (see also Küchenhoff 2006b).

Mr A. grew up in tight domestic circumstances in a lower-middle-class family in a Swiss village. Because of the Second World War the patient's father had to break off his studies and had to bury his wishes and ambitions of a higher education. He was forced to look after and eventually take over the family's meagre and impoverished agricultural business. All this contributed to the fact that the patient's father became more and more silent until all of his vigour and passion had died down. What always stuck in Mr A.'s memory is the image of a father sitting motionless at a heavy wooden table in a somewhat dark room. The father's family and the father's sister, the patient's aunt, come from a village in the mountains (a fact that will play a momentous role in the patient's later life). The mother's family of origin lived in the valley. And like the patient's father his mother too grew up in humble and poor surroundings. Although the educational standard of the father's family of origin was considerably higher than that of the mother's, this difference did not appear so significant anymore after the father's failure, that is, his enforced abandonment of his professional and educational ambitions. According to the patient's account, it was the mother, who looked after the children and took care of them like one takes care of plants that have to be cultivated and watered, so that they grow and find the approval of the neighbours. Mr A. later on in his life could not recall any instance of physical closeness, nor any display of affection or kindness.

The patient calls his aunt the most important figure and – to a certain extent at least – a source of inspiration in his life. The patient's aunt kept a shop, in which among many other things she sold books. This gave the patient, when he grew up, the opportunity to discover that there are actually 'people in this world, who have a passion and love for thinking'. And his aunt was also the only person who, in spite of her otherwise rather strict and austere attitude, showed some affection towards the patient and genuine interest in his life.

Mr A. has two brothers. One of them has developed an addictive disorder, that is, he has spent most of his life drinking alcohol. The patient says about his brother that he is 'a notorious womaniser unable to go out to work and totally unable to hold on to any gainful employment'. The patient's other brother never left his native village. He earns his living working as a craftsman and uses a part of his parent's house as some kind of storing place for his small handicraft business. He is the only one of Mr A's siblings who has a family of his own.

During the patient's childhood and youth, there seems to have been no room for otherness in the patient's home environment. At some time during puberty Mr A. becomes rebellious. He decides to take up a technical, not an agricultural apprenticeship. He refuses to participate in or take over the father's agricultural business and decides to leave the parental home against the will of his father and mother, who both are unable or perhaps unwilling to understand their son. After the completion of his apprenticeship he cannot find an employment and comes under increasing financial strain, so that he has to resort to move back into his parents' house. The moment he enters the parental home, the scornful laughter of his father roars in his ears.

Once again Mr A. makes efforts to live his own life, that is, his otherness. Thanks to his high intelligence and his talent for languages the possibility opens up for him to complete his *abitur* through second-chance education. He then studies at the university, he radicalises himself and becomes a member of extreme left-wing groups, and after that travels to China following the tracks of Mao. He burns his bridges behind himself living a life where there seems for him no way back.

At that time he makes a lot of friends. With some of them he keeps in contact over many years. In the course of the therapeutic conversations during the sessions it becomes more and more apparent that there are two types of relationships to women that specifically matter to him: one type is the earthbound and motherly woman, the other type is the intellectual and autonomous female partner. In his search for a mate he constantly oscillates between these two types of women. The woman who later would become his wife does not fit either type of woman. At best she might be described as the type of a failed intellectual, whom he would wish to give help and support in whatever way he can. It might well be that she reminded him of himself before he was given the opportunity to pursue higher education and a career via the second educational pathway.

Every now and then during his studies Mr A. returns home to his parents, ruefully offering his apologies and begging them for forgiveness for something which exceeds his parents' coping capacities and which they do understand no more than they do understand their son's overall way of living. In a family, which lives a totally norm-oriented life and whose members have all lapsed into silence, and in which the children are cultivated like plants and looked after in an almost mechanical manner, are granted absolutely no room for freedom and no room to move, and are supplied with no more support and understanding than is necessary to carve out a miserable existence, it certainly does not come as a surprise that any aspiration of a family member moving into the direction of personal development is deemed an offense against the invisible and silent covenant between the family members.

After the completion of his studies Mr A. becomes a teacher. Shortly before that he had married and started a family with the intention to find his own way of life and to now become himself a father and adopt a paternal role – and this is what marks the onset of a progressive change within himself, which is lasting about a year. Astonishingly, nobody seems to notice it, not even his psychiatrist he sees

56 Psychoanalytic theories about psychosis

from time to time for treatment because he suffers from a depression. Soon danger lurks behind every corner, and Mr A. can everywhere descry an uprising of the maternal, of the earth and the water, which revolt against the sublime, the masculine and the spiritual. He therefore seeks to avoid everything in his everyday life that might equip the feminine principle with ever more power and influence.

None of the people surrounding him seems to realise that Mr A. is about to undergo a dramatic change. And nobody realises that he increasingly changes his habits. For instance, that he would put up with long detours in order to avoid driving his car through villages bearing a female name or otherwise hinting at something feminine. Furthermore, he can no longer open an Apple computer without first executing a complicated and cumbersome ritual, because the bitten-into apple on the notebook lid evokes the Fall of Man and Paradise. Aside from that, he no longer dares to go to a public swimming pool because the pull of the water has now become so intense that he is afraid that the waters might engulf him, swallow him up and never again release him. At the same time, he is an attentive father towards his young daughter and he treats his wife, who is a young mother, in such a way that nothing strikes her as unusual about him.

Not before long he can see appearing on the computer screen written messages that are only meant for him and which cannot be printed out. Only he is able to see and read them on the computer screen. Soon he is convinced that these written messages are divine commands: it is him who was chosen to save the mountains from the valleys, the land from the waters, the spirit from the maternal. In order to fulfil the task predestined for him in the approaching Apocalypse he then, even leaving aside his usual moderate manner and caution, starts planning and subsequently executing violent actions. And that is the point in time when he eventually turns himself over to the police – and when he afterwards lapses into complete silence. He subsequently is diagnosed as schizophrenic and arrangements are made for a long-term hospitalisation and psychiatric treatment.

It is during his long stay in the clinic that I start seeing him in a psychotherapeutic setting. I had been asked to treat him in individual therapy, because he was considered 'insupportable'. The sessions with him are very demanding because he remains silent most of the time. I am almost entirely left to my own devices, only making use of my own counter-transference feelings and phantasies and only, in the midst of the shared silence, from time to time letting the patient know what I think he might be feeling at the moment. There are times when I, too, would prefer to pursue the path of least resistance and label him with the diagnosis of unchangeable defect resulting from acute paranoid-hallucinatory schizophrenia. But then, suddenly, there is something that catches my attention. Among the few words Mr A. says to me, there is a self-description that strikes me as extraordinary: 'I am an inmate.'

From then on I try to look at him as an inmate, which finally helps me to come to understand and recognise the falling silent of Mr A. as an attempt at restitution: as a last resort to somehow save his subjectivity, to re-gain his own language. And so taking Mr A. seriously as an inmate finally allows me to conceive of Mr A's self-designation 'inmate' as a signifier referring to a subject. But what exactly does this mean: to be an inmate? Gradually different layers of meaning emerge, at first in my counter-transference feelings and then also within the therapeutic conversations with Mr A. And thus I come to understand 'to be an inmate' means:

- Self-definition of one's own subjectivity: What appears first of all significant is the 'I am', whereby the attribution of a property ('inmate') is perhaps only secondary. Understood in this way, it can be concluded that Mr A. thus for the first time after his psychotic breakdown perceived himself as a person.
- The restitution of an order. After the long psychotic breakdown and the dissolution of the internal order and the subsequent construction of a psychotic, self-enclosed delusional order, the statement 'I am an inmate' means also the awareness of an external, shared order, which must be recognised.
- Self-condemnation: Gradually it becomes evident that this formula 'I am an inmate' implies also an enormous and devastating guilt feeling. In this sense the formula 'to be an inmate' means to be infinitely and forever guilty and to have forfeited the right to any other decent and civic existence.

Another layer of meaning of the formula 'I am an inmate' refers to the patient's object-relationships. It reveals the patient's failed attempt at an identification with the father whom the patient during his childhood experienced as an inmate in his own house, and who had condemned himself to silence after he had had to give up his ambitions of a better life and an higher education. At some point in time during his extended therapy Mr A.'s father dies. The passing away of his father seems to leave the patient completely indifferent, and he also does not attend the father's funeral.

And so it has been possible, in a psychotherapy that lasted more than a decade, to work out the patient's life-determining issues, which also provide us with the opportunity to reach a more profound understanding of schizophrenia. It became more and more evident that the problem of the recognition of otherness (cf. Küchenhoff 2005) has always been central to Mr A's life. The right to self-determination and independence was not only condemned in the patient's family of origin, but was not even given voice to and thus remained beyond the realm of possibility. Where there is no room for difference, language is absent, because language is based on the recognition of difference.

In the terminology of the Lacanian theory of psychosis (cf. Küchenhoff and Warsitz 2017) one could say that the paternal signifier had been foreclosed in the case of Mr A.: he cannot be a father himself, he cannot be autonomous, something he always had been striving for throughout his entire life; when he eventually becomes a father in the biological sense, and also in the symbolical sense, for instance, in becoming a teacher, this marks the onset of his schizophrenic delusion which undermines the basis of his existence. Mr A. , whose otherness had always been denied, now becomes in actuality an 'other' through schizophrenic decompensation, which marks him permanently with the stigma of 'otherness' or 'alienness'.

The tragic thing about the psychotic process is that it even widens the gap between the actual external reality and the schizophrenic's endeavour at restitution in the desperate attempt to fill the empty spaces inside and thus reach some kind of secondary healing. And for that reason we have to conclude that in real life Mr A. destroys his hard-fought-for, yet never symbolically inscribed otherness, his successfully won acknowledgement as intellectual, as father and husband, who is capable of dealing with gender difference productively. However, in his delusion something completely different becomes manifest: he is driven to put a halt to the threatening overwhelming power of the forces of nature, of the feminine and the amorphous – and thus the imaginations of violence serve the function of safeguarding a difference, which is experienced as being gravely at risk. The psychotic phantasy serves the purpose of delaying the imminent end of the world, the drowning in a world of undifferentiated chaos – thereby reversing in reality the life-long hard-earned differentiation, that is, the process of becoming and being another.

Sigmund Freud put forward the hypothesis – and Lacan would take this as point of departure for his theory of the psychoses – that in psychosis what was abolished internally returns from without (Freud 1911: 71; Lacan 1993: 46). In the psychotic experience the family members become the concrete, de-symbolised embodiments of an immemorial revenge, the revenge of wordless nature on the word, which betrays nature; in this particular case, it is the mother's revenge on her son, who surpasses her and leaves her behind, etc. But something essential is reversed or undone in psychotic experience: the recognition of difference.

The significance of destructiveness in psychosis

Wilfred R. Bion has called our attention to the fact that hatred is a decisive factor in the development of psychosis, which will re-emerge in the transference where it has to be recognised and worked through in the course of the analytic process. Herbert Rosenfeld, for his part, was convinced that psychotic patients are, contrary to the claims of some of his colleagues, capable of developing a transference relationship, but argued that transference in the case of patients with psychotic disorders was of a more concrete nature. Holding on to his firm belief in the analytic process, Rosenfeld recommended to apply the therapeutic technique of simply analysing and interpreting the patient's transference feelings and his sadism, projected into the therapist, and not to respond with reassurance or other attempts to support the patient, because this ultimately prevents the development of the analytic process.

Rosenfeld (1964, 1987) describes – and here he departs from Melanie Klein's conceptualisations – a specific form of pathological splitting in psychotic patients that differs from that in patients with a severe personality disorder. In the case of pathological splitting the normal and structuring splitting between 'good' and 'bad' breaks down, which subsequently leads to unbearable states of confusion and depersonalisation resulting from destructive attacks mounted against the 'good' object itself, so that it ultimately becomes impossible – libidinally as well as aggressively – to distinguish 'good' from 'bad'.

Why is it that the recovery of the psychotically ill person is so incredibly difficult to achieve? With regard to this Rosenfeld comes up with an answer in that he describes these personalities as being in the domineering grip of a 'mafia-like gang', a destructive organisation, which he understood as a manifestation of the death instinct. Unlike in ordinary narcissism in destructive or negative narcissism, as Rosenfeld called it, the libido gets under the omnipotent and domineering sway of the death instinct and destructiveness is idealised and libidinally cathected. Rosenfeld finds plenty of clinical evidence for this destructive narcissism in his patients, in which part of the personality is organised solely for the purpose of the expression of death instinct impulses and manifests clinically as an idealisation of destructiveness and an attack on the subject's own good parts, an inner state of affairs that has the capacity to take over the entire personality. Rosenfeld looks for and finds evidence of this scene of an internal battle that has been lost, especially in his patients' dreams of being attacked by members of the mafia or by a gang of hooligans and subsequently giving in to and being completely taken over by their aggressive, brutal and anti-life demands.

The pathological organisation of destructive narcissism takes the shape of the idealisation of the 'bad' parts of the self, often represented as a mafia gang. Whereas in libidinal narcissism there is an idealisation built on the idea of absolute union, in pathological narcissism there is a 'mad' self-idealisation and like in every mafia-like organisation its highest ideal is the total destruction: what's absolutely forbidden is any libidinal impulse, or any search for the good object because there is an inner censor, a kind of negative counterpart to the ego-ideal that watches over the absolute adherence to the destructive tendencies. In contemporary psychoanalysis it is seen as one of the most challenging tasks to adequately deal with destructive narcissism in the psychoanalytic treatment today. Rosenfeld's last book *Impasse and Interpretation* (1987) is in this respect an important guideline, and can be considered as a further development of Freud's description of narcissism as the turning of the libido towards the ego in an act of self-love, while Rosenfeld introduced the notion 'negative narcissism' to describe an internal state of the ego's destructiveness towards itself.

What Rosenfeld describes as destructive narcissism is something similar André Green (1986) aims at with his description of the relation between Eros and Thanatos, characteristically defined through the relation to the object, not because Green considers the relationship to the object as primary in line with object relations theory, but rather because he takes the view that the drive only becomes manifest through the relation to the object, as the drive always seeks satisfaction by means of the object, albeit never being wholly successful in this. Green suggests that the life instincts serve an objectalising function, that is, the function to establish an object relationship, which allows to cathect the object. The death instinct, by contrast, manifests itself through a de-objectalising function, that is, through the attack on the object, but also through the attack on the cathexis of

60 Psychoanalytic theories about psychosis

structure itself, for instance, of language and finally on the processes of cathexis in general: the death instinct thus aims at the dissolution of processes of binding, 'attacks on linking', and the withdrawal of libidinal cathexis. In other words, Green argues that the function of the life instinct is to sustain a tension, or a difference, in relation to the object, whereas the function of the death instinct is to abolish or destroy this tension or difference.

Thus Green's concept of narcissism (1983) seems to be of great relevance in this context here: Although the libidinal narcissism recognises the difference to the object, its last aim is the obliteration of the trace of the Other in one's desire, which leads to the abolition, or at least reduction, of the difference between One and the Other, in that consequently a distinction will only be made between enemy and friend. The aim of negative narcissism is then the abolition of tension to zero-level, and, consequently, the abolition of all the differences. What above has been described from a drive psychological perspective as an acceptance or a defence against an experience of difference, now in the light of the more recent concept of narcissism brings into question more explicitly the recognition of the difference to the Other. It can be said therefore that also from an intersubjective perspective the awareness and acceptance of the experience of difference is considered to play a decisive role.

Experiental spaces and the development of representation

That it requires time and a specific mode of experience to negotiate difference in a playful way, even more, to first of all develop the capacity to play, this is a discovery we owe to D. W. Winnicott. Winnicott's admonition 'Do not challenge!' inscribed over the entrance to the transitional space evokes that all those who enter here must not abandon all hope but the belief in the logic of identity. Whether the cuddle cloth belongs to the self or to the object, this is a question that must not be asked, but must be accepted as a paradox. The transitional experience is an experience in the neutral area of experience and is creative because it allows for repeating Freud's fort-da game, that is, it allows for the playful negotiation of presence and absence which produces internal images that help tolerate the feeling of abandonment (Winnicott 1971).

Transitional experiences are basic to the development of representations and symbol formation. It essentially requires a certain distance between self and other, that is, an intermediate area that allows for the representation of experience. But one can, of course, also look at it from a reverse perspective: If a world of representations, that is, a symbolic order is formed, then this creates a certain distance between the self and the world, between the self and the other, who in a certain sense always represents a rupture in the immediate experience of reality but, nevertheless, is also the guarantor of a potential space.

Transitional spaces with their creative potential must be distinguished from so-called 'psychic retreats' (Steiner 1993), which are enclosed, non-productive areas of withdrawal, that is, pathological inner spaces which are defence organisations against narrowing object relationships. In psychosis this may mean the withdrawal into an isolated delusional world. The delusional world is idealised for the reason that it affords the psychotic individual protection against psychotic anxieties of disintegration and annihilation.

Although the use of the metaphor of space has acquired such high significance in the psychoanalytic discourse, it should not be forgotten that it is nothing more than just a metaphor. Experiential spaces develop on the basis of mental processing of experiences of separation and of lack. This leads us directly to one of the most important concepts in psychoanalytic theory, that is, the concept of triangulation which refers to the core complex of the neuroses: the Oedipus complex. If the child becomes aware that his or her primary attachment figure has emotional ties to other people as well, the child's phantasies of omnipotence are challenged: the primary attachment figure is not omnipotent, but is itself in need and dependent upon others. Furthermore, the child is not the sole source of maternal or paternal satisfaction; the parents have a sexual life the child is excluded from.

A lot more could be said with respect to the child's experiences of relativisation in the context of triangulation. Suffice it at this point to refer to the peculiar double meaning of the word 'relativisation', which may provide us with some more insight into this complex matter. Relativisation includes the word 'relation', which refers to a relatedness of some sort. But relativisation means also the opposite of absolutisation. And hence triangulation is a form of relativisation: awareness of relatedness under the condition of incompleteness. And this is the reason why triangulation is the paradigmatic model for the formation of human experience. The Kleinian psychoanalyst Ron Britton (1998) therefore points out that the child's capacity to tolerate in his or her own mind that the parental couple is having a life of its own is the necessary prerequisite for triangulation which is in turn the requirement for symbolic thinking. This, however, requires an active effort on the part of the child to move away from the world of dual relationships and the related phantasies of omnipotence and grandiosity. For the individual prone to psychosis this is an almost impossible task to achieve, but in the same breath one has to also say, it is definitely made difficult for him or her.

Pathological narcissism and the defence against triangulation

The French psychiatrist and psychoanalyst Paul-Claude Racamier (1982) dedicated himself primarily to the psychotherapy of schizophrenic patients. Racamier's original way of thinking, firmly anchored in his own clinical practice, and his keen spirit of 'going further' in his clinical work with psychotic patients as well as in his theoretical writings is especially evident in his conception of the 'Antoedipus', a constellation, which is according to Racamier typical for the schizophrenic patient. This phantasm is an obstacle to the oedipal organisation and, as a corollary of that, any awareness of generational differences or of procreation are radically cancelled out. Oedipus, the prototypical hero of psychoanalysis, must recognise that he has unknowingly married his mother and killed his father. And with this recognition the difference between the generations is reinstated, albeit it entails that Oedipus must now accuse and punish himself.

With the concept of the 'Antoedipus' Racamier describes a phantasm, a fundamental pattern or tendency in human beings which is, however, particularly characteristic of the psychotic personality: generational differences as well as the fact of begetting and along with it any kind of dependency are negated and denied. The 'Antoedipus' is his own begetter, father and son simultaneously. In this sense the phantasm of the Antoedipus is a reflection of early omnipotence, a pathological form of narcissism, in that it cancels out all boundaries and all sexual and generational differences. One might also say, what is typical for the Antoedipus is the resistance against the recognition of the three 'facts of life', as described by Roger Money-Kyrle (1981: 443): the recognition of the breast as a supremely good object, the recognition of the parents' intercourse as a supremely creative act and the recognition of the inevitability of time and ultimately death. The basic denial is thus directed against any form of dependence, whereby any form of separation- and castration anxiety is avoided and replaced by the idea of self-creation, and the idea of being the father's father, and of being the begetter or creator of oneself.

This position has been quite accurately described by Giorgio Sacerdoti: The Antoedipal phantasy aims at healing the wounds, which have been inflicted upon the subject by the recognition of filiation (i.e. of being the descendant of the object). And now the 'phantasy of self-generation' comes to play a major role as powerful antidote against this recognition, which contains the idea of generating and begetting, even though in the sense that the sequence of filiation has become reversed, with the effect of being literally some kind of self-made man. 'The subject takes the place of his own parents and places itself before and prior to them thus rendering the parents ineffective. With it sexual difference is annulled' (Sacerdoti 1990: 751). What is described here is a phantasy which sends the psyche back to a primitive and pre-object world where there aren't yet any internal mental images or representations. This produces an overall situation of complete denial, particularly of the fact that one owes one's life to one's parents.

If a psychotically ill person is caught up in such a delusional world dominated by the Antoedipal phantasm this implies not only that any awareness or recognition of dependency but also of triangulation is radically cancelled out. The phantasy of being one's own creator is equivalent to the phantasy of being a godlike creature. This involves an unavoidable misrecognition, with the effect that there is no such thing as lack or deficiency in one's own life. The Antoedipal hero is neither in need of self-enlightenment like Oedipus, nor is he in need of any help or assistance from other people, which means he lives a life that follows exclusively its own rules and laws beyond any imagination of what it could mean to have gratitude for other people or to perhaps envy them.

The concept of the Antoedipus gives us some idea of how deep an abyss someone may fall into, when he or she is at some point in his life going beyond the resistance characteristic of the 'Antoedipal' psychotic experience, that is, when

Psychoanalytic theories about psychosis   63

the patient has to finally recognise and accept that he is actually dependent on medication, on psychotherapeutic treatment and on the assistance and support provided by social or community workers. Although the patient may find that there are ways of overcoming the resistance and going beyond it, we as therapists can hardly expect from the patient, when he is thus engaged in the working through of these pathways, any feelings of gratitude – if only perhaps as an indication of the patient's capacity to now have an awareness of the importance of the significant other – because too immense and too incisive is the suffering and pain which the patient's going beyond the resistances and the concomitant fall into an abyss elicit. Now when considering this, it certainly allows us to better understand and appreciate why in some cases there is such an enormous 'resistance' against any form of active participation or cooperation in the therapeutic process, and which cannot be overcome for a very long time, in some patients even throughout their entire life.

Psychotic solutions to basic conflicts of human relationships

Stavros Mentzos (2009) emphasises the functional nature of psychic symptoms: He conceives of psychic processes of the psychotic patient not as determinate phenomena indicating a fatal and unremoveable defect, but rather understands them as having an object-seeking function. This finalistic view with regard to the symptom immediately suggests the question: What does the patient attempt to achieve by developing a specific symptom? But this implies also the assumption of the patient having an – albeit perhaps unconscious – intention. In other words: the patient is actively seeking something in developing a specific symptom. Viewed from this perspective, one could say that the patient does not merely suffer from psychosis, but also produces it.

This approach is more or less in line with the above descriptions of the various psychoanalytic theories and conceptualisations of psychosis, even though it should be taken into account that Mentzos's approach is not focussed upon the deficits of the symptoms. This finalistic view takes a certain aspect even further and thus concentrates on the important task to not only determine the cause of the symptom, but rather to recognise and make use of the productive function of the symptom, which also means to establish contact with the motives that are responsible for developing the symptomatic behaviour in first place. One could therefore argue that the approach proposed by Mentzos is consistent with the psychoanalytic psychology of conflict insofar as he attempts to once again take it as the basis for the psychodynamics lying at the core of all psychic disturbances. His anthropological basic assumption is that human beings are by nature bipolar. What this basically means is: they are dominated and driven by opposite tendencies or impulses. But Mentzos is not merely focussing on the conflict *per se*, but he holds the view that it is time to focus on an until now somewhat neglected aspect, which is, nevertheless, decisive for the development of the patient's psychic suffering,

64 Psychoanalytic theories about psychosis

that is, the specific form or mode of the defence, because Mentzos starts from the premise of the symptoms bearing a productive function.

This approach has the advantage that Mentzos can discover similarities between otherwise very different psychic symptomatologies. Mentzos demonstrates that psychic disturbances often are complementary and alternative reactions to similar basic problems or basic conflicts. The discovery of these isomorphisms or homologies led Mentzos to the conclusion that putting this conception of the symptoms into practice would mean to develop a comparative psychodynamics. And yet Mentzos avoids to valorise or devalorise other concepts, but rather prefers to bring them into a fruitful dialogue. For instance:

- Trauma versus conflict: Mentzos stresses the point that early traumatisation in itself does not necessarily account for the development of psychopathology in later adult life. But it is more appropriate to consider trauma as being responsible for the fact that the basic human conflicts cannot be adequately dealt with and worked out in later life. Thus Mentzos concludes that the defence strategies against and the modes of dealing with conflict of the adult patient have to be closely examined as this allows the clinician to draw conclusions about the original trauma. And so the defences and defence strategies employed in response to the trauma are viewed to have their own history.
- Conflict versus structural deficiency: Mentzos considers deficits not as primary phenomena, but rather as secondary ones in that they represent inadequate solutions to basic conflicts.
- Psychiatric classification and psychodynamic diagnostics: Mentzos does not strictly oppose psychiatric classification, but he finds fault with it, because he is convinced that it needs to be renewed and supplemented with a psychodynamic approach. He even makes a plea for a 'psychodynamisation of the diagnoses'.

There are specific basic conflicts or dilemmas of human life, which revolve around the development of one's own identity (how to preserve and protect the self and, at the same time, to establish and maintain contact with others) and, furthermore, around the constitution of self-worth or self-value (how to get individual and durable ways of self-esteem through creating a connection with others). This immediately raises the question: what are the psychotic 'solutions' to these basic human conflicts?

At the core of schizophrenic psychoses lies the dilemma to find a solution to the conflict of being neither too close to nor too distant from the object, since being too close involves fusion danger and persecutory anxiety and being too distant involves terrible loneliness and loss of contact with the object. The schizophrenic personality's solution to the dilemma of the attractive power of the object and its dangerous impact on the self is typically dealt with in that the object is ignored or minimised – whereas the self becomes inflated and held in high esteem to the detriment of the object-dependency. Another alternative solution we frequently encounter in cases of hebephrenic schizophrenia is to succumb to the attractive power of the objects (father and mother), which involves a blurring of the boundaries between self and object or even complete fusion with the object.

The other basic conflict addressed by Stavros Mentzos concerns the ambivalence of the ascription of value: on the one side, there is the constitution of self-value and, on the other, the recognition of the value of the object. This dilemma is characteristic for the condition of bipolar disorders: the manic patient who enters a manic phase tends to minimise the value of the other, whereas patients during the depressive phase typically resort to self-denigration.

Stavros Mentzos's concept is not so much significant in terms of making a major contribution to nosology, because he frequently draws upon what has already been described and elaborated in the context of other theoretical approaches. But putting his specific understanding of the psychotic symptomatology in practice has proven to be of great advantage in developing a clinically promising therapeutic attitude towards the psychotic patient in particular: the therapist's implicit assumption is that the psychotic patient's specific symptomatology is built upon an intention, has a purpose; and so the therapist tries to not only acknowledge the patient's suffering but, beyond that, to understand the defensive function of the productive symptoms oscillating between object-seeking and object-avoiding in the patient's desperate attempt at finding a solution to the difficult conflict of the dialectical pair of object-neediness and self-safety. This therapeutic approach has the invaluable advantage that both therapist and patient are given the opportunity to become increasingly aware of the fact that they are actually not dealing with an unchangeable, fatal defect but with a conflict that also becomes manifest in the therapeutic relationship and thus offers them the opportunity of working with and overcoming this conflict, or perhaps simply finding an alternative and better solution to it. This approach proposed by Stavros Mentzos brings us back to everyday psychiatric practice, where the clinician is confronted with the task of bringing to bear the various psychodynamic approaches for the benefit of his or her patients.

Positivisation as a basic therapeutic attitude

The therapeutic and scientific work of Gaetano Benedetti, which is primarily focussed upon 'the psychiatric patient as our fellow human being' (*'Der Geisteskranke als Mitmensch'*; Benedetti 2002), points in a similar direction to the work of Stavros Mentzos. Central to Benedetti's approach is his idea of 'positivisation', a concept he developed in the course of his extensive psychotherapeutic work with psychotic patients.

Basic to this concept of the 'positivisation' of the psychotic experience is a different understanding of and approach to psychopathology, extending psychopathology to new horizons and thus leaving behind a psychopathology degenerated to mere description however operationally refined. One of Benedetti's main concerns is to interrelate the patient's clinical symptomatology with what happens in his mind and with what the patient is trying to accomplish within himself and in society, in other words, the patient's personal project of life. Benedetti is the only psychopathologist who discovered and subsequently made a passionate plea for a therapeutic and progressive potential within psychopathology itself. In line with this the concept of positivisation describes a basic therapeutic attitude, pushing towards the 'positivisation' of the psychotic experience by absorbing and identifying with the catastrophe occurring within the patient and thereby neither objectifying nor denying the patient's suffering. The notion of 'positivisation' is well chosen in that it refers to two different aspects: first, *all* of the patient's expressions and communications deserve to gain the therapist's attentive awareness and acceptance; and, second, therapeutic positivisation means that the therapist absorbs and introjects all of the negative or deficient parts of the patient and by way of psychically metabolising them transforms them into something meaningful with the objective of reaching a more positive, anti-psychotic 'position' within himself. And so, by the therapist's concentrating on the patient's suffering in his presence, this suffering is not doubled but rather made available for re-introjection as something new and more positive.

Benedetti distinguishes between seven different types of positivisation of the patient's psychotic experience. The first type is dedicated to 'life-historical identity research' which does not mean to uncover and hence interpret unconscious complexes and conflicts but rather to learn on the basis of the therapist's empathic identification with the patient something about the history of the patient's violations of his self-boundaries, which is a basic conflict to be faced by all human beings, but which concerns the schizophrenic personality in a very particular way. According to Benedetti the aim is an 'expanded experience of subjectivity': The therapist is there with the intention to mirror the identity of the patient and, furthermore, the identity the patient creates in the intrapsychic space of the therapist emerging out of the therapeutic-dialogical interweave of the therapeutic relationship. And thus the hope is that the patient rediscovers his own boundaries and his own self in the therapist, because previously the self has become alien and a stranger to itself due to compulsively reiterated intersubjective conflicts particularly with regard to boundary violations. Now, the assumption is that it is only by the emotions of the intersubjective relationship and the re-experiencing of those basic conflicts that the self may eventually regain a more coherent and enduring self-identity.

The second type of positivisation refers to the 'corrective phantasies and free associations of the therapist' and is intertwined and interdependent with the first type in that the patient's experience, or perhaps more precisely, the centre of the patient's self that pours out and spreads itself projectively outside, can only be modified and transformed by the therapist's own phantasy activities within the framework of the interpersonal therapeutic relationship. This, obviously, brings Benedetti's concept of positivisation in close proximity to Bion's model of the container/contained.

As we can see, both types of positivisation arise from a shared experience of the therapeutic relationship, that is, from the therapist's participation in the patient's subjectivity, particular of those parts of it that are too great a burden to be carried by the patient alone. So what positivisation aims at are the loss of ego boundaries and the patient's excessive need for externalisation and projection. Subjective experience is made available to the patient if the therapist has the strength to sustain and recognise inside of himself the patient's negativised parts and idiosyncratic expressions of subjectivity in order to then 'give them back' to the patient in a new and positivised form.

As far as the third and fourth type of positivisation are concerned, one has to first state that 'communicative psychopathology' implies that the therapist recognises in the psychotic symptom the productive and antipsychotic intention, in other words, the latent creative potential that can be made use of in the course of the therapeutic process. To phrase it differently, besides making use of his own reaction to the patient, the therapist also conceives of the patient's symptom as a form of creatively expressing his own subjectivity, however buried under the patient's overall negativism. In any case, it is of crucial importance that the therapist in the therapeutic empathic identification with the patient can take over the patient's existence lost in the desert of his psychosis. To achieve this, the therapist does not only take over the patient's explicit language but also attempts to assess and hence name the patient's implicit, non-verbal language, in order to communicate to the patient that he is the author and creator of all of his experiences and that all of his expressions including his symptoms have a meaning, not only for the other as detached observer, but even more so and in particular for the patient himself. The patient's language is thus appreciated as his own interpretation of himself and the world he lives in. Communicative psychopathology viewed in this light can thus be said to conceive of psychopathology as a vehicle of communication and not as an index of a destroyed interior world. To what extent this communicative positivisation has been lost in the last few years or decades can be gathered from some of the consequences of the introduction of the contemporary concept of 'disorder', because we could already witness in recent years how the concept of disorder subverted what had already been achieved. So it is fair to say that the concept of disorder does, in effect, contribute to the re-pathologising of the symptom.

The fourth type of positivisation in the therapy of psychosis refers to the therapist's sympathetic and empathic understanding of the patient's psychotic experiences and expressions as a form of 'identification with the patient' that may lead to the creation of a specific transitional experience, a 'transitional subject', between patient and therapist and which is rooted in both persons and subsequently assimilated, bit by bit, by the patient. Benedetti emphasises that in this common production of shared empathic and emotional experience the patient is not seen as a passive recipient, but is always recognised as an active participant with a communicative intention and productive potential. It can be said that this is an essential component of every form of psychoanalytic psychotherapy in that the fourth type of positivisation focusses upon the *poietic* (i.e. the creative or even poetic element in psychotherapy). In that sense any transitional experience is an experience of shared creativity.

Benedetti has repeatedly shown that the identification with the psychotic experience of the schizophrenic patient does not only demand from the therapist a great deal of courage but that, beyond this, the therapist's ability to let himself be transformed by it may also have a profoundly deepening and enriching effect upon the therapist. The progressive and modern character of Benedetti's approach of positivisation is striking, particularly if one considers that the creative aspects of the psychotherapeutic process have recently been intensively and extensively discussed. Benedetti's emphasis on the communicative approach in psychotherapy where the interdependence of patient and therapist lays the foundations of a new kind of intersubjectivity that may lead to the creation of a new self-identity of the patient and possibly also of the therapist, brings to mind Thomas H. Ogden's concept of the 'analytic third' (Ogden 1994) which emerges out of the dialogic experience of the therapeutic relationship.

The other three types of positivisation are: (i) The negotiation and mediation of the patient's resistances, his non-understanding, and his loss of contact; (ii) the getting in touch and identifying with the catastrophes occurring within the patient to rediscover the tragic life experiences responsible for the patient's symptomatology; and finally (iii) the forming of creative and transforming images of the patient's destructiveness and psychic deadness. Viewed in this way positivisation means neither downplaying nor euphemising these negative parts of the patient, nor does it mean some kind of positive thinking. What it needs, though, is the therapist's readiness to be with the patient in his world of destructiveness and death, which implies the therapist's constant endeavour of gaining therapeutic awareness especially of all of the negative aspects of the patient including his ideas on death and the tragic events of his life. This requires, first and foremost, the therapist's capacity to sustain, often for a very long time, these negative sides, without condemning or even counter-reacting to them. And it is this therapeutic attitude which actually enables the therapist to establish even closer contact with his patient.

At this point Gaetano Benedetti's line of thinking brings to mind Money-Kyrle's idea of the 'facts of life', which I already referred to further above. All too often we as therapists fail to recognise the creative potential inherent in destructiveness and consequently we might think it is imperative to fight it. Perhaps we are still not clear enough in our minds – notwithstanding the clinical necessity to occasionally prevent the acting out of destructiveness – that in some cases the only way for the patient to hold on to and protect his own self is to resort to destructiveness. The therapeutic work with anorexic female patients can give us an idea of how closely intertwined death and autonomy can be. But dealing with destructiveness means also that we as therapists must be prepared to face up together with the patient to the tragic and catastrophic events of his life or illness without shading the facts and without endowing them with 'undue meaning', but rather to develop the strength to sustain and contain them.

Chapter 3

Conditions of psychotic experience

A psychodynamic factor model

Preconditions

The selective overview of the various psychoanalytic theories of psychosis I have outlined in the previous chapters of this book might provide us with a better understanding of the meaning and relevance of these psychoanalytic theories for the purpose of developing psychotherapeutic techniques particularly suited for the treatment of psychotic patients. The fate of the different psychoanalytic conceptualisations, developed over the last decades or more, follows a similar course as other theoretical discourses in philosophy or in the cultural sciences: notwithstanding the positive effects and benefits of each single approach there comes a time, when due to the ongoing theoretical debates the older and previously developed models, which are permanently kept under close scrutiny, may not exactly prove obsolete and useless, but cannot keep up any longer with the constantly evolving research landscape and constantly changing perception of reality, which creates a situation that inevitably brings forth important new questions and problems. And yet, we should not forget that it was also and perhaps mainly due to the positive effects of these older models that these new questions could finally materialise. The point I am making is: despite their limitations these previously developed psychoanalytic models are still not yet completely obsolete and we cannot just put them aside once and for all, only for the reason that they are a hundred years old or even more.

The metaphor of a scientific house may help clarify what is at issue here. No single theory can claim this house for itself alone, in which the psychoanalytic and psychodynamic theory of the psychoses resides. There are many parties residing in this house. Each one has a right to exist and live in this house, and arguably no one has the claim to sole representation. Now, one possibility would be that the different parties fight each other and blame each other for betraying the common idea of the shared house or for producing too much waste or perhaps loud noise, etc. It goes without saying that such an ongoing quarrel sooner or later makes life for the various parties living under the same roof impossible. So, the other possibility would be that the house community cooperates in managing the concerns of the house and tries to settle all of the emerging conflicts and problems with mutual respect.

70 Conditions of psychotic experience

What I would like to suggest is that in such a house, so to speak, resides the factor model of the psychotic disorder. The aim of the factor model is therefore not to present a new theory, but rather to provide a model that combines and carefully considers the interrelation of the different relevant areas – marked-out in the text below – in order to tackle the serious challenges thrown up by the complex issue of how to understand and treat the psychoses.

Formal structure of the factor model

The psychodynamic factor model of psychotic experience is not supposed to serve the purpose of providing a synopsis of the various above-described approaches. Rather, those approaches are taken as launching points in order to now be in a better position to reflect upon and get clear about the preconditions of normal psychic development and the resultant constitution of mental capacities, which in case of a psychotic disorder are either non-existent or gravely impaired or deficient. With this in mind we are going to first address and consider the preconditions of normal psychic development. They can be divided into the following categories:

- *Subjective experience:* the reference here is to a phenomenology of experience and the related developmental stages. Hereby the following elements are of relevance:
  - the recognition of the basic facts of life in psychic development,
  - the differentiation of the relationship between self and object,
  - the integration of the drives,
  - the quality of bodily experience.

- *Objectifiable mental capacities:* Apart from the subjective experience there have to be also taken into account the 'objective' factors, that is, the preconditions that are not necessarily revealing themselves in the subjective experience of the subject, but which are, nevertheless, a basic requirement for the development of the aforementioned levels of psychic experience to be accomplished in normal psychic development. These include:
  - the integration of ego-functions or the ego's structuralising and organising capacities,
  - the capacity to represent experiences.

- *Quality of object-relationships:* And finally, there is to be considered the quality of the early object-relationships made available to the subject from as early on as infancy. Admittedly, this normally can only be inferred from the analysand's subjective accounts, but it is, nonetheless, important that the therapist gets a somewhat clear idea about the quality of the early object-relationships of his/her patient. What therefore has to be taken into account is:

- the specific quality of the relationships provided by the attachment figures (i.e. the significant others).

All of these factors of normal psychic development are then, in each section, considered in relation to the psychotic experience. For the sake of clarity in the presentation of the factor model, I have decided to only briefly refer to the relevant areas, but not address them in any sustained detail. The model is purely designed to enable a more far-reaching and well-grounded understanding of the complex interaction of the preconditions of the psychodynamics of psychosis.

Preconditions of psychotic disorders

The various preconditions for the psychotic experience are deduced from three main factors, which are first described in general terms to then assess their special relevance for the psychotic experience. These main factors are the subjective experience of the psychotic patient, his objectifiable psychic capacities, and finally the specific quality of his early object-relationships.

Subjective experience

The recognition of the basic facts of life

Psychic development, if it's going well, is based upon the recognition of the basic facts of life (Money-Kyrle 1981). Among these are:

- The recognition of the succession of generations, and along with it the fact that one is the creation of one's own parents. All of this implies to accept and not deny the fact that one's life has an origin and an end, which are ultimately and definitely uncontrollable events.
- The recognition of dependence, that is, the recognition of the protecting and nurturing function of the other.
- The recognition of separateness and separation, that is, the recognition of the inevitability of the passage of time and ultimately of death.
- The recognition of the impossibility of being the master of one's own desires and impulses, so ultimately, of the impossibility of being the master of one's own unconscious, which can never be completely resolved by consciousness: The ego is not 'the master in its own house'.

We know of course that the denial, disavowal and non-recognition of 'the facts of life', and along with it the denial of the necessity of development, plays a major role in psychosis. One therefore could state that most characteristic for the psychotic experience is a development- and life-negating tendency.

72 Conditions of psychotic experience

With the myth of the 'Antoedipus' Racamier has described the schizophrenic phantasma of being a son, who has begotten himself, which basically refers to a regressive tendency typical for the psychotic experience, namely to the idea of self-generation. What thus is denied is the dependence of one's own existence upon one's parents. The inevitable consequence of this is that there will be no negotiations or mediations with the parents, since the important role the parents play in one's own psychic development has to be radically repudiated and denied in the service of psychotic withdrawal.

But not only the succession of generations is denied. What is also denied is the dependence on others, although this seems scarcely possible, because in actuality we are more or less all of the time confronted with other people. Yet, only if one is able to be aware of and appreciate that the other person possesses desirable human traits and capabilities, the recognition of the other becomes a realistic possibility. However, if there is too much envy of the other person's potency and value, this will all the more aggravate and intensify the denial of dependency, because envy invariably aims at destroying the superiority of the other. And thus one can say that manic defence is directed against any form of dependency.

Most illuminating in this context is the study of the various types of the so-called residual disorders, but also of some forms of schizophrenia like hebephrenia or schizophrenia simplex. The essential characteristics of these conditions can best be grasped and understood by way of analysing and studying the patient's subjective time experience. As it appears, these patients are anti-temporal: time has virtually come to a standstill and the patient radically denies the progression of time. And this in turn entails that any form of development is resisted against and foreclosed. But it still leaves the central question unanswered, why the psychotic patient has to eliminate the recognition of the passage of time, which after all prohibits any personal or psychic development.

The solution to produce delusional ideas or images of 'something being done to oneself' (delusion of reference or persecution), very often related to a sexual idea or phantasy, is a way of mastering the origins of the libidinal impulses and desires because: if my desire is perceived as being influenced and governed by the other, then this also means that the sexual or libidinal impulses have no longer to be recognised as being a part of my own psychic endowment and of my own personality. It is thus via the creation of a delusion, which basically serves the function of denying the origins of sexuality that a specific modification in the subject's mind is brought about, so that the subject can now once again reign – at least partially – over his own unconscious impulses: so we can see that it is paradoxically this activation of the delusional phantasy of being influenced by others that enables the subject to make himself or herself again the 'master of his or her own house', even though by way of a short-cut or detour.

The differentiation of the relationships between self and object

Psychic development can be conceived of as a continual psychic growth process constituted by the gradual differentiation between self and other in one's own

Conditions of psychotic experience 73

experience. This involves a fragile and precarious equilibrium forever threatened by collapse and situated between the following opposite poles of experience:

- over-proximity to or fusion with the object including loss of ego-boundaries versus isolation, loss of contact, and loneliness;
- cathexis of the object versus perception and recognition of the otherness of the object or other;
- cathexis of the object versus cathexis of one's own self (object-love versus self-love); and
- love of the object versus the wish to destroy the object (libido versus destructiveness).

It seems that the psychotic individual can hardly sustain or tolerate the dialectical tension situated between the opposite poles of fusion with the object *and* loss of contact with the object or loneliness, that is: possessing the object (cathexis) *and* letting go of the object (recognition); self-love *and* object-love; love *and* destructiveness. If these opposite poles are experienced as irreconcilable psychic positions, this inevitably gives rise to the psyche's urgent struggle against any form of development, because if this is actually the case the idea of development amounts to the idea of eternal ending, of total loss, of loneliness and isolation, and a separation beyond which no life is deemed possible any more. The destruction of the object in phantasy cannot be compensated for or overcome through the survival of the object, as Winnicott described it (cf. Küchenhoff 2005), but inflicts seemingly irreconcilable harm and damage on the object, so that the total withdrawal from the object in the service of self-protection and preservation of one's own boundaries seems to be the only escape route. This, however, entails the denial of temporality. In psychotic experience time has virtually come to a standstill, since beyond the mediating function provided by a viable object relationship, everything, that is, in particular any loss or lack, has to be immediately denied since in this situation nothing can be negotiated or playfully dealt with any more in an in-between area or potential space, which is, after all, a basic precondition of any psychic development.

André Green (1997) described what he called the separation-intrusion dilemma, particularly encountered in the '*cas-limites*', the borderline-cases, which confront the psychoanalyst with serious problems that raise technical questions about analysability. Stavros Mentzos described as a characteristic and common feature of the different psychotic disorders the patient's struggle to find a solution to a basic human conflict, namely to keep a distance from the object and yet, at the same time, to establish and maintain a contact with it. The different psychotic disorders confront the clinician with both extremes: a fusional relationship with the object that may go so far that in phantasy there seems to exist no boundary between self and other (for example in cases of hebephrenic patients), or else, withdrawal from the object and the retreat into total isolation in one's own delusional phantasy world.

74 Conditions of psychotic experience

Already for the neurotic the recognition of the other is a huge challenge, for reasons that are attributable to the fact that the libidinal cathexis of the object is necessarily always fraught with uncertainty, tension and conflict. But in sharp contrast to the neurotic patient, for whom the question is about how to resolve this problem, for the psychotic patient, who is struggling against massive persecutory anxieties and the fact of the uncontrollability and inaccessibility of the object, the challenge would be just to avoid entirely having to face this problem of object-seeking and object-neediness. And so, for the psychotic personality, there seems to be much at stake in the resolution of this basic conflict or basic dilemma, since he may experience the cathecting of the object as so extremely threatening and dangerous that very often de-cathexis and total withdrawal from the object seems to be the only way out of this dilemma.

The annihilation anxiety experienced by the psychotic patient and his grappling with the most harrowing anxieties of losing his boundaries and separateness from the object is thus correlative with the de-cathexis of the object and the concomitant over-cathexis of the self, employed by the psyche to compensate for the object-loss. In the attempt to describe the psychic mechanisms of de-cathexis, which is a typical feature of the loss of the object in psychosis, André Green proposed the 'deobjectalising function', which according to Green aims at destroying all relational links to the object.

For André Green the deobjectalising function is closely connected with the unbinding of the death drive, which in psychosis seems the only way out from a fusional relationship with the primal object. In other words: if, as is often the case in psychotic patients, the love of the object as well as the aggressive impulses towards it, cannot be tolerated, they will be deposited in, that is, projected into the object. As a corollary of this, the libidinal or aggressive impulses can no longer be recognised as being part of one's own experience but as coming from outside, that is, from the object – with the result that the psychotic person in his world of amorous or persecutory delusions has reinstated a relationship with this now over-cathected object, albeit a delusional one.

Integration of the drives

To come to terms with one's own drive impulses that are always more or less incompatible with one's own conscious intentions and which can only slightly be translated into consciousness and verbal language, appears to be a life-long and highly challenging learning process, which implies:

- The recognition of the impossibility to be the master of one's own desires and wishes, which means that life is basically unpredictable and incalculable and that one's thoughts and actions are very often not governed by conscious intentions.
- The libidinal and destructive tendencies have to be recognised and accepted. If they remain largely a taboo subject psychic integration will inevitably be jeopardised.

- Normally there is a fusion of libidinal and destructive impulses. In this – however permanently fragile and precarious – equilibrium the libidinal tendencies ought to outbalance the destructive ones.
- Regulation of drive impulses is essential; over-regulation as well as under-regulation has a detrimental effect and causes problems.
- The drive manifests itself in its relation to the object. That's why the quality of the object relationship is an index of the degree of integration of the libidinal impulses.

The libidinal and destructive tendencies often undergo a process of decomposition in psychotic experience, which accounts for the fact of idealisation or repudiation of parts of the self or of the object. The constitutional strength of the destructive impulses, which then have to be dealt with by a poorly integrated ego, can equally have negative effects, since this may lead to an ever growing disproportion between the capacity and the necessity of mental processing.

Freud's analysis of the Schreber case was based on the assumption that the homosexual tendencies could not be accepted and thus had to be repudiated and disowned by way of projection. The same applies especially to the destructive impulses. If they are experienced as too destructive and hence extremely frightening, they have to be disavowed, expelled and projected into the object.

It is not without reason that the battle between good and evil is a recurrent theme in the delusions of the psychotic. The imminent end of the world refers to the existential crisis of the psychotic patient: in a last apocalyptic battle the good rises up against the evil, heaven rises up against earth or hell, man against woman and so forth, in order to save the good – very often the delusional patient is charged with a redeeming mission and – in his mind – is chosen to perform a task which is unique and specific.

The manic psychotic patient loses all inhibitions and self-control, and hence desires and urges are acted out regardless of the consequences. In the case of the catatonic psychotic patient, by contrast, all impulses for action are extremely obstructed, and in the case of catatonic stupor they are totally immobilised.

The quality of bodily experience

In studying the development of self-experience, a central role must be allocated to the examination of the way in which the subject relates to his or her body. In this respect the following criteria are of particular relevance:

- Integration: How integrated or fragmented is the bodily experience?
- The relationship between bodily experience and psychic experience: How dependent or independent are psychic and bodily experience from each other (they may be either too undifferentiated or too dissociated from each other)?
- Aliveness: How and to what extent is the body emotionally cathected?
- Functionalisation: Is the psyche seeking support from the body in the service of defence?

76 Conditions of psychotic experience

In the case of psychotic patients the clinicians or therapists often encounter a lack of cohesion in their patients' bodily experience. This involves a dissociation of the body image, in which parts of the body lose their link to the whole and may also be experienced as no longer related with one another, and subsequently reappear as detached body parts in the outside world, sometimes in the guise of visual hallucinations. This makes them appear particularly uncanny, frequently causing hypochondriacal anxieties. Gisela Pankow (1975) in her seminal work on the treatment of psychosis suggested with regard to the dissociation of the body image that the first function of the body image makes it possible to recognise a dynamic link between the various parts of the body and the whole, a function which in most psychotic patients is apparently missing or deficient. In some cases there may occur a re-cathexis of the body in that parts of one's own body reappear in the external word in the form of a hallucination or in the guise of a visual delusion.

That the aliveness of the felt body in psychotic experience may at times be drastically diminished or even totally obliterated finds evidence in the catatonic patient. The same applies to the patient suffering from a severe psychotic depression, in which case the nihilistic delusion can even go so far that the body is no longer recognised by the patient as his or her own.

In the attempt at regaining access to one's own bodily experience, there may occur an over-cathexis of the body, which indicates the psyche's desperate attempt to seek support from the body in order to limit, contain and organise the self. And this perhaps explains why some psychotic patients have to resort to self-harming behaviour. Viewed from this perspective, these seemingly bizarre and terrifying self-inflicted injuries are not to be considered as destructive but rather as a desperate attempt at literally seeking support of the body's skin in order to once again feel oneself and one's own body.

This shows that the level of bodily experience can have an ambivalent effect. The loss of personal identity, that is, the loss of a coherent self-image may manifest itself in the inability of experiencing one's own body as a unity. The patient's subsequent over-cathecting of his or her own body can thus be understood as a first attempt at re-connecting with the felt body, or in other words, it may be viewed as the patient's attempt at reintegration. When therapeutically working with these patients, particular care should be taken to ensure that the therapist takes over the verbal language, the patient him- or herself uses to refer to, comment upon or describe his or her symptomatology. Or put differently, naming the imaginary body of psychosis has to be considered a vital therapeutic action that initiates and keeps alive a creative process, in that the therapist conveys to the psychotic patient that his/her subjective experience is appreciated and taken seriously, not in the sense that it is taken as the absolute truth, but rather to let the patient know that a third and more detached view is possible, which may pave the path for further moving on in the therapeutic process into the direction of the creation of a more symbolic and representational world.

Mr C. is a 20-year-old man, who had hit on the idea of making seafaring his career. First indications of an emerging decompensation could be observed, when during his maritime training he had to embark on a long sea journey lasting several months. It seemed impossible to him to tolerate the radical separation from his family, but equally the feelings of being trapped in a pure male world of sailors on board of the ship. And so it proved to be a virtually insurmountable challenge for Mr C. to adjust to the contrast of proximity and distance: on the one hand the radical distance from his family of origin, and on the other, the enormous proximity to the crew on board of the ship. We know the following data from his life: When Mr C. was six years old his parents separated. The father was overly expansive with little or no critical introspection; the mother was overly emotional, although, at the same time, depressive. When Mr C. was two years old an orchidopexy was performed on him to resolve a testicular torsion (orchidopexy is a surgery to move an undescended testicle into the scrotum and permanently fix it there). Mr C. was in the midst of a psychotic breakdown, when it was suggested by his doctors that he should undergo surgery because of a suspected testicular torsion (the spermatic cord rotates and cuts off blood flow to the testicles). It was his psychiatrist, who 'saved' him from having to undergo surgery, because he was fortunately able to make the accurate diagnosis of 'coenaesthesia'. The patient described his condition in the following words: 'The organs in my body have slipped.'

It is important to note that Mr C. in his own understanding did not make use of a metaphor – for him it was a matter of fact that his organs inside of his body had slipped and thus gotten out of place. He could virtually sense and feel it in his body, in particular the testicular torsion, which had assumed the quality of a bodily hallucination. Unlike the patient, the therapist is then able to conceive of the patient's words as definitely having a metaphorical meaning, and consequently also manages to bring to bear its therapeutic potential: the therapist understands that due to the radical breaking away from the parental home, which obviously greatly exceeded the patient's psychic capacities, he subsequently had the feeling that the life, as he knew it, was actually 'slipping' away from him. But the therapist also understands that the overwhelming anxieties of the two-year-old boy, who had to have an operation, because it was deemed necessary to surgically displace the testicles into the scrotum, now at this particular point in his life returned in the guise of the psychotic delusional belief that the organs in his body, but especially his testicles, had 'slipped'.

So now the question arises: Who is capable of setting things – that is the distorted organs in his body – right this time? It becomes more and more obvious that the search for the father as representative of the male body plays a major role for Mr C.'s experiencing his self-identity as a man – but the very moment this search for the identification-object becomes sexualised, the patient is prone to homophobia.

78 Conditions of psychotic experience

The objectifiable psychic capacities

The integration of the ego-functions or the psyche's organising capacities

The ego-functions pertaining to the 'mental apparatus' are a prerequisite for the development of psychic experience. It should be recalled that the issue here is not to resolve the question, if these ego-functions are innate and genetically determined or if, as a consequence of deficiencies in the subject's early object-relationships, they could not or merely insufficiently be developed due to a lack of suitable identification objects or role models. Foremost among these ego-functions are:

- Perceptual capacities:

  - Self-perception and external perception can be affectively charged and processed to a varying degree.
  - Perception requires filtering and distancing from the objects.

- The capacity for regulation:

  - Drive regulation (see above).
  - Tolerance of negative affects is an index of a balanced and healthy affective life.

- Level of the defensive functions:

  - Are the objects used in the service of safeguarding the defence ('interpersonal defence')?
  - Do neurotic defence mechanisms prevail (according to the concept of repression), or rather the defence mechanisms of splitting or foreclosure?

According to the 'Operationalised Psychodynamic Diagnostics' (OPD), in psychotic experience the differentiated perception of the object is abolished, if the object is only ever perceived from the perspective of the persecutory object. The same applies to cases of over-cathexis or under-cathexis of the self which manifest as megalomania or as self-denigration or guilty self-accusation in the case of a depression.

Equally important are the ego's filter functions which are more or less absent in the preliminary stages of psychotic decompensation, a mental state which is then experienced by the individual as agonisingly threatening. Werner Janzarik, one of the last great psychopathologists, coined the term 'impressive disinhibition', by which he described a state of mind where the boundaries between self and others are blurred and hence the sensual impressions that normally remain preconscious invade consciousness: the sensual impressions urge themselves unfiltered into the psychic field, because they cannot be linked with other sensual impressions and therefore cannot be turned into something that holds emotional meaning.

Conditions of psychotic experience   79

The issue of drive regulation was already referred to in more detail further above. For the psychotic patient affect-regulation invariably poses a major problem. Whereas the depressive patient is haunted by feelings of guilt and self-incrimination, the alcohol addict, who develops a delusion, finds himself compelled to lock all doors and windows in order to protect himself from the looks and assaults of the outside world. The latter type of patient will not be reassured and will not calm down unless concrete measures are taken. The patient's delusional belief arises out of his incapacity to emotionally distance himself from his delusional experiences.

Jacques Lacan describes foreclosure as a specifically psychotic defence mechanism. Lacan phrases his insight in his own terms: 'what is refused and not inscribed in the symbolic order [. . .] reappears in the real' (Lacan 1993: 13). With this Lacan refers to an essential distinction between repression, where that what was experienced and subsequently suppressed internally becomes unconscious, and foreclosure, where that what was abolished internally returns form without. So, whereas in case of projection, the direction of the process is from inside to outside, in case of foreclosure the foreclosed element returns from outside. And hence the voice, for instance, is no longer recognised as one's own and inner voice and allocated to the subject, but the voice is now allocated to somebody else, coming from without – or, as Lacan put it, reappearing in the real. This amounts to a radical expropriation of one's inner representation, as a corollary of which, it cannot be linked with other representations and thus not be mentally processed or metabolised.

The capacity to represent experiences

The development of language and speech is here referred to as an independent factor, although it is, of course, closely linked with all the other factors. The development of language and speech is predicated upon the quality of the object-relationships and ego-functions as well as upon the development and integration of the libidinal and destructive drives. But due to its paramount importance the topic of language and speech development deserves its own special section.

The development of language and speech involves the following dimensions:

- *Representation of experiences:* Can the lived experiences be represented and psychically processed or are they foreclosed (i.e. rejected) outside the symbolic order just as if they had never existed?
- *Linkage of experiences:* Can the represented experiences be linked with each other or are they dissociated and do have to be kept apart or split off from each other? Are word-presentations and thing-presentations bound together, or are signifier and signified held apart and disconnected?
- *Formation of experience:* Are there reference persons, or significant others, who can help create and form new experiences (through containment and reverie etc.)? Can the experiences (of separation and frustration) be tolerated and thus mentally digested or not?

80 Conditions of psychotic experience

- *Psychic spaces:* Does the quality of the development of psychic representations allow for the creation of inner spaces of experience (i.e. of intermediate spaces of phantasy), which are relatively independent so as not to be contaminated or destroyed by the various external adverse influences?

The language and speech disorders in psychotic experience are indications that there is a total or partial failure to accomplish the psychic task of representing experiences and integrating them in a symbolic system. 'Foreclosure' is the *terminus technicus* that refers to the subject's incapacity to integrate certain fundamental experiences into the psychic structure, as for example the identification with the third.

Characteristic for psychotic experience are the 'attacks on linking' (Bion 1959), as described by Wilfred R. Bion. The detrimental result is an invasion or intrusion of separate, unlinked elements of experience (beta elements). These failures of inter-linking and cross-linking of signifiers can be compared to the phenomenon known as 'impressive disinhibition', the concept introduced by Werner Janzarik, and described in more detail further above in the section on perceptual changes in psychosis. Another important issue in all this is the question of destructiveness, which Bion accounts for with his concept of 'attacks on linking'. The significant and massive lack of phantasy in a residual condition may be indicative of a mental activity serving the function of protecting and safeguarding the self from objects experienced as too intrusive.

Traumatic representations typically cannot be linked to other representations and thus cannot be mentally digested or 'experienced', as a corollary of which they remain unaffected and timeless and can neither be repressed nor forgotten. This is an important issue in the analysis of the life history of the psychotic patient and thus the question has to be raised: What role do the un-assimilated experiences play, which could not be integrated and which resemble mental implants of bad objects which could not be assimilated into the psyche?

That a person can start making experiences, this requires the provision of a transitional space. In order to represent these experiences it then needs an in-between space that guarantees a balance between distance and relatedness to the object. Objects that are too intrusive fail to provide the space or freedom necessary for making experiences and for representing these experiences. The same applies to the so-called dead objects. André Green's concept of the 'dead mother' (Green 1983) comes to mind, who is physically present but, at the same time, psychically absent – and therefore unable to guarantee protection.

The quality of object relationships

Development depends upon the quality of object relationships made available by the infant's environment. The specific quality of object relatedness of the significant others, who are not merely objects, but nevertheless present themselves as objects, plays a decisive role for the development of self-experience. Now, what

Conditions of psychotic experience 81

are the specific functions to be fulfilled by the significant others or attachment figures? These functions include:

- the quality of the object-relationships, which recognise and respect the boundaries between self and other, but which also allow for experiencing these boundaries and are not denying nor disregarding them;
- the function of reverie (i.e. a dream-like thinking state), which has the function to intuitively understand the infant's or patient's needs within the frame of the relationship;
- the function of containment (i.e. the receiving, containing and metabolising of experiences), which includes the possibility to experience lack and loss in a safe and protected environment in order to thus learn to tolerate and to digest experiences of separation, etc.;
- the function of representation (i.e. the naming of experiences in order to help create representations of these experiences that could be made within the frame of the relationship); and
- allowing for transitional experiences through repeatedly providing for a transitional space.

So, when considering and carefully reflecting upon the complex interaction of the preconditions of the psychodynamics of psychotic experience we must be fully aware and always keep in mind that there are – as we have just outlined above – several 'objective' factors resulting from the interaction between an environment (quality of object relationships provided by the attachment figures) and a personality, especially in the early stages of the infant's psychic development. In other words, besides the innate characteristics of the child ('subjective' factors), there are also the additional 'objective' factors that are essential preconditions for a person to be prone to psychosis later in life.

The repeated violations of boundaries in the early object-relationships prevent the development of spaces necessary for the creation of representations. But even if the boundary violations are seemingly not so severe, but rather subtle, in that the boundaries between the subject and the other family members are blurred because the issue of separateness and difference is not sufficiently encouraged and dealt with, this can equally cause more or less severe problems. But if there is too much distance, this may be detrimental too, as it leads to isolation, loneliness and loss of contact.

The function of reverie necessarily relies upon the existence of a relational space which has to be 'well-aired'. Transitional spaces should neither be too limited, nor too broad in scope, since both might contribute to the impossibility to make experiences. At times when the growing child or adolescent is confronted with challenging threshold situations and the related emotional and developmental demands, it is particularly important that the significant others make themselves available to the child's or adolescent's subjective experience with their more mature and more integrated symbolic universe of phantasies and wishes to help

82 Conditions of psychotic experience

the child or adolescent to make his or her own experiences in order to create and link representations.

In all stages of psychic development the experience of containment is essential. For a long time the importance and significance of the period of adolescence for the psychic development was in a certain respect underestimated. But today it has become commonly accepted that also and especially the time of adolescence with the adolescent child's striving for independence, autonomy and self-identity is an essential developmental stage for making experiences and particularly for the formation of a representational world. This is invariably a highly challenging time for the attachment figures, because now it will be their task to ensure that the adolescent child can make his/her own experiences in regard to loss and separation, which are experienced as acceptable and not too intolerable, albeit this may often prove to be a particularly painful experience for the adults or parents themselves. However, the capacity of the reference persons to come to terms with and endure such experiences of separation plays a decisive role not only during the child's adolescence but throughout the child's entire childhood. Containment implies always also an understanding approach towards the child's aggressive tendencies, his attacks and his efforts to distance himself and draw boundaries between himself and the Other.

No child is born into a pre-symbolic universe. From the very beginning the child lives in a social network that has already been initiated by the previously existing symbolic order. One significant function of the reference person is to verbalise the emotional content of the child's experiences. By naming what the child encounters in the world and within the frame of the immediate relationship, the reference persons will help the child to create representations of his own experiences and in that way a process is initiated that enables the child to construct a symbolic order and a symbolic world of his own. Viewed from this perspective, one could argue that the semantic gaps and empty spaces in the symbolic universe of the person prone to psychosis later on in life, may be due to the early attachment figures' failure of providing the function of naming, in other words, the failure to introduce the child into the symbolic order.

If we stress at this point the important role played by the significant others and the quality of early object-relationships, we should, at the same time, be careful not to fall prey to gross over-simplification, since this may lead to unfounded accusations. If we take into account all of the different factors operative in the self and in the other, we will find that there is a complex interplay of all these various factors, where some factors might compensate for others, or even make good the damage caused by the other factors. The following three paradigmatic constellations may illustrate this point:

- If an intensely aggressive drive endowment is dealt with by a strong ego respectively by early reliable attachment figures who make themselves available to help metabolise the infant's experiences, this may compensate for the subject's innate aggressive drive endowment, which is, of course, not the case

Conditions of psychotic experience 83

if the subject happens to come across a failing, deficient, perhaps resentful and retaliatory environment.

- If the child grows up in an overly intrusive environment, which does not grant the child the possibility to experience frustration within tolerable limits or which does not allow the child to experience the direct impact of boundaries and limits, while at the same time leaving room for grappling with the challenge of frustrations and disappointments, this can have a detrimental effect upon the child's overall speech and language development, which is predominantly based on the capacity of representing one's own experiences. However, a child with a strong aggressive potential, equipped with an eager and lively mind, inclined towards the exploration of the environment, as a corollary of which the child can create a distance and draw boundaries around himself, will be less affected by over-protective or intrusive attachment figures than a child with a more passive and dependent character.
- If the primary attachment figures merely provide for a one-dimensional relationship experience and negate, punish and even actively eliminate the other side of the dimension of experience, this will create a situation in which the acceptance of the conflictual nature of experience is made impossible. In such a case alternative reference persons – such as grandparents or siblings, but later-on in life also teachers etc. – may play a substantial role in making available to the growing child alternative relationship experiences.

It bears repeating that the purpose of the factor model is to first describe and reflect upon the various preconditions for normal psychic development and the resultant constitution of mental capacities and of identity-structure or personality-structure. These preconditions of normal psychic development are then, in a second step, considered in relation to the psychotic experience. Even though perhaps not all of the described factors are equally important in the therapeutic encounter with the psychotic patient, the clinician or therapist might, nonetheless, profit from bearing in mind the various factors presented in this factor model in order to help create the conditions for building a bridge between those – possibly – two very different worlds of clinician and psychotic patient.

Conclusions from the factor model

The necessity of a multidimensional understanding of psychosis

The phenomenon of psychosis mystifies and profoundly unsettles us. We don't know what the psychotic person is up to in the conduct of his life. Meeting with the psychotically ill individual immediately challenges our hoped-for hold on things, on the basis of which we – all of whom neither afflicted and burdened with a psychotic disorder nor having an idea what it means to undergo psychiatric treatment – usually can pursue our day-to-day activities without consciously being

84 Conditions of psychotic experience

too worried about life's necessities and its utilitarian demands. Even though there has been a considerable change of mentality in large parts of society, which has brought in its wake a steady decrease of stigmatisation of the psychotic or mentally ill person, and even though a rapid removal or efficient reduction of symptoms through the availability of psychotropic drugs has become possible, the human suffering due to a psychotic disorder can still be enormous. In either case, it is important to recognise that psychotic disorders still mystify us and the enigma of the psychotic disorders is still unresolved and reliably effective forms of therapy or treatment methods have not yet been developed and are still only a hope for the future. And this applies equally for the neurobiological as well as for the social-psychiatric and psychodynamic approaches.

Due to the complexity of the psychotic disorders anything but a treatment approach in a multi-field therapeutic–diagnostic institution with their multi-professional team under specialist medical leadership will fall short of the requirements of providing a satisfactory solution to this problem of the appropriate treatment of psychoses. So far none of the treatment approaches has developed a reliably effective method that can guarantee optimal treatment results. On the evidence of this still very unsatisfactory situation there is indisputably a need for a special sensitivity, tolerance, respect and modesty which concerns all of the therapeutic groups. And this applies just as well for the different psychoanalytic approaches, even though it is to be stressed especially that we cannot manage without them, if it is our foremost and main concern to truly understand our patients and thus provide improved and efficient treatment for them.

So what we have just been discussing has to not only be emphasised in view of the numerous psychiatric–psychotherapeutic treatment methods but also in view of the more specified field of the various psychoanalytic approaches. We have to become more comfortable living with the idea that any one-dimensional approach within the wide spectrum of psychodynamic theories and therapies of psychosis must fall short of what is actually needed to understand and treat patients who suffer from psychotic disorders. There is a wide range of factors and preconditions that have to be assessed and subsequently put in relation to one another. The factor model presented in this chapter may help to pay closer attention to what is actually going on in the psychotic patient's psychic world and to possibly observe certain essential aspects previously not sufficiently considered or reflected upon. There are a great many factors worth considering as preconditions for the development and aetiology of a psychotic disorder, which is always mostly the result of several factors convening and then influencing and mutually reinforcing one another. And that's why we as therapists of the various psychotic disorders are always confronted with a complex set of interdependent conditions, where no part of it can be adequately described or understood in isolation. This certainly also carries implications for the therapeutic work with the psychotic patient. Three examples are given below to show what is meant by the complex structure of interweaving conditions:

- If the subject's constitutional strength of the drives (i.e. his innate drive endowment) is exceedingly strong, in particular with regard to the destructive tendencies, it is essential that the object is able to provide a containing function in order to facilitate the formation of experiences.

- If the attachment figures, or significant others, are unable to set boundaries, this will inevitably have as a consequence that the possibility of experiencing separateness and accepting the 'facts of life' is considerably minimised and restricted.
- The more affect control and the better the perceptual filter function, the more the subject will be relatively independent of the protective and 'metabolising' function of the object, in other words, even if the containing function of the primary attachment figures is gravely deficient this will under these particular conditions not have such a detrimental effect on the subject.

Viewed from this angle psychotic disorders are the result of relational problems and conflicts, and thus can be considered as having – at least partly, even though perhaps not wholly or exclusively – their origin in failed or traumatising relationships. But they do, in any case, become manifest in the relationship with other people, and will most certainly always have a huge impact on these relationships later in life. As therapists we should seriously and carefully consider this relational perspective, which then may serve us as a basis for developing a generally supportive and adequate therapeutic attitude to optimally help patients with a psychotic disorder.

In that sense, it is important for both, therapist and patient, to become aware of the fact that in case of a psychotic disorder, they are not merely dealing with a fatal and unremoveable defect or deficiency, but rather with a difficult conflict or dilemma. And thus, although psychotic symptomatology is invariably deeply distressing and unsettling and often persistent due to its primary or secondary morbid gain, this does not mean that the treatment of psychotic symptoms inevitably implies a hopeless struggle against an unchangeable defect. Any symptom has to be also conceived of as the patient's attempt at self-restitution, because therapeutic technique can profit from these self-healing tendencies and processes. The productive symptoms became especially evident in the Schreber case, where the delusion finally appeared as *weltenaufgang* ('rise of the world') and not as the end of the world.

Persons with a psychotic disorder entertain a more specific relationship to the universe of language and verbal representations than other people. Any symptom has a communicative function which has, however, to first be understood, translated and interpreted by the therapist. In the case of the individual prone to psychosis there is an apparent vulnerability of the symbolic universe, because he or she has never been properly introduced into the symbolic order. The therapeutic technique of translating or interpreting psychotic experiences therefore essentially implies to name whatever the therapist manages to assess of the direct personal relation and its libidinal or destructive qualities, and what the patient so far has failed to make part of a symbolic universe shared with other people.

Speech and language disorders are always closely linked with relational disorders, a situation which is commonly the result of a complex interaction of influencing factors already described in more detail further above. According to D. W. Winnicott, the provision of a 'good enough' relationship that allows for the oscillation between symbiosis and separation, enhances symbol formation and thus verbal representations. Conversely, it could also be said that the capacity to form representations and the capacity to mentally digest and reflect upon one's own experiences are essential factors in establishing and maintaining vital relationships to others.

The psychotherapist's basic attitude in working psychodynamically with psychotic patients

Just as in any psychoanalytically based psychotherapy, the treatment concept is also in the encounter and therapeutic work with psychotic patients based on the patient's relying on a solid and functioning relationship serving as the launching point for the possible future work with the patient.

The aim of psychotherapy is not to merely concentrate on the pathological aspect of the symptom in order to then try to repair it, but rather to find the life-enhancing potentialities contained within the dynamics of every psychotic symptomatology. It is certainly a huge challenge for us as therapists to understand and accept the specific relationship with the psychotic patient, which implies to share the patient's suffering and anguish inherent in his experience of living, while setting aside our own individual value system. But this is precisely what Gaetano Benedetti's concept of positivisation actually means: the therapist's recognition and acceptance of the adaptive value of the psychotic symptom formation as a necessary solution to a basic conflict, which the patient could just not find another or better solution to, and which all too often and all too easily is just dismissed by the clinician or therapist as some kind of 'disorder' and thus prevented from bringing to bear its latent creative and therapeutic potential.

'Positivisation' therefore also means that the therapist must accept reaching the patient only within and by his symptoms, that is, using his symptoms as necessary channels through which to approach the patient and his subjectivity. But although it is true that the therapist has to try to establish contact with the symbolic meaning of the patient's symptoms, as long as the patient can only express himself through his symptomatology and not yet sufficiently through symbols that are part of a symbolic universe shared with others, this does, however, not mean that the patient's subjectivity is something hidden inside or within the symptom that can be revealed and translated through the therapist's intellectual operation, or, put differently, that can be interpreted and made conscious. A psychotherapy that adheres to the principle of 'positivisation' favours a basically communicative approach, whereby the therapist recognises the interdependence of the patient-therapist relationship, and thus lays the foundation of a new kind of intersubjectivity in that the patient's subjectivity may eventually in due time grow and develop. One could even say that the therapist has to be prepared to acknowledge some radical forms of acting or even acting-out, for example, acts of self-harm and

Conditions of psychotic experience 87

self-injury, but also the hearing of voices etc., as subjective forms of self-realisation and hence ultimately as a creation of subjectivity. It is precisely the therapist who does not try to take the symptoms away from the patient, but lives with the patient together with his symptoms as long as it is necessary that is, reacts emotionally to the kind of affects contained in the symptoms, who thus conveys – at least implicitly – to the patient that, firstly, he recognises and appreciates the patient's subjectivity which is still contained and concealed in his symptoms, and which the patient himself cannot yet live and experience; and, secondly, that he understands the patient's symptoms as an attempt at self-constitution.

Relational dynamics and psychotic experience

What are the specific advantages of a psychodynamic approach in view of achieving optimal therapeutic results in working with psychotic patients?

Just as in any other psychoanalytic psychotherapy the working with and the working through of the psychotic patient's transference plays a decisive role. The difference is that in case of the neurotic patient the focus lies on resolving and working through neurotic conflicts, whereas in case of the psychotic patient the working through of the transference is primarily concerned with mental patterns and defence mechanisms closely connected with the dissolution or blurring of boundaries between self and other, which makes it necessary to deal with massive projections and introjections. Due to the loss of the symbolic order and the subsequent blurring of boundaries between self and other in the patient's psychotic experience the work of the transference will necessarily bring these boundaries between self and other into focus. But, at the same time, the therapeutic work has to also call the patient's attention to the recognition of the 'facts of life', so that the therapeutic effort may hopefully lead to the patient's eventually giving up of his resistance against any form of change, and along with it, the giving up of the psychotic imagination of a timeless and limitless therapeutic space. One has to emphasise at this point that it is important that the interpretation of the psychotic experiences must be carefully considered, so that the patient still always feels contained and not mentally and emotionally over-burdened or stressed, in order to then become able to metabolise and finally integrate the various emotional therapeutic experiences.

There are cases, however, where something else than verbal interventions or interpretations is needed in order to bridge or heal the profound gaps or holes in the symbolic world of the psychotic patient, as for example, body work (Küchenhoff and Warsitz 1993) or art therapy (Pankow 1975). But indeed sometimes verbal interaction will successfully lead to the re-introduction of a symbolic structure that previously has been lost. In any case, the therapeutic effort always aims at the reversal of foreclosure of the symbolic order, which is a basic precondition for experiencing boundaries between self and other. Now and then this can actually be achieved through a simple 'no' leading to a form of structuring (i.e. a triangulation and thus the introduction of the symbolic order), which not only sets up

88 Conditions of psychotic experience

boundaries, but which, at the same time, helps mentally digest and integrate the painful experience of now having to tolerate and come to terms with these boundaries. The following example may illustrate this point:

> Mr B. is 20 years old. He was diagnosed with a hebephrenic schizophrenia and subsequently has been treated in the psychotherapy department for first episode psychotic patients for a considerable length of time. It didn't take long until Mr B.'s family dynamics became apparent. The still youthful looking mother raised her son alone. During her son's stay in the clinic she comes for a visit on a daily basis, each time staying for several hours. In the course of one of the conversations with a member of the team on the ward she then reveals an intimate detail: when growing up her son was always afraid to sleep alone at night in his bed and that's why the mother allowed him to sleep next to her in the same bed. This situation of intimate closeness to the mother often aroused the son's sexual excitement to such an extent that it then led to the son's excessive masturbatory activities in order to discharge the high level of sexual tension. Now, the mother not only tolerated her son's behaviour but, on top of it, provided her son regularly with paper tissues, which she afterwards disposed of in the toilet.
>
> The team on the ward subsequently makes the decision to prohibit the mother from coming to see her son more than once a week and allows her never to stay longer than for a one-hour visit. The mother vehemently complains to the director of the clinic, but to no avail. This selective and targeted measure has an amazing effect upon the patient, who in the course of the following months gives up his jejune and stifling indifference towards the passing of time and even starts actively participating in the rehab program of the ward.

However, often this kind of structuring or triangulation cannot be accomplished in the therapeutic work with psychotic patients, which always endeavours to move into the direction of the recognition and acceptance of the 'facts of life' and the inevitable experiences of lack and loss. In such cases it may prove beneficial to make use of the fact that the ego is first and foremost a body ego, which means that it has its origin in the body. If it should be the case that a maximum of physical presence is asked for by the patient, the therapeutic technique may have to resort to either direct 'body work' or else the patient's 'body image', a therapeutic method which makes use of the patient's ability to project his body image on to objects, as, for instance, in Gisela Pankow's modelling technique, which allows for a dynamic 'structuring of the body', making shapes with clay (Pankow 1975; von Armin et al. 2007).

The inpatient psychotherapy treatment of psychosis, which utilises the ward and its specific environment as a therapeutic factor, offers the patient the opportunity to project his psychotic anxieties and catastrophic fears on to the ward-as-a-body. The therapeutic team has to then contain, synthesise and reflect upon its own inner relational dynamics, so that the patient can eventually re-introject the team's catalysing and synthesising function, which will not only bring about the reduction of psychotic fears but, most significantly, the formation of new representations on the basis of the patient's experiences of containment (Küchenhoff 1998). Here, it can be said that the therapeutic work primarily pursues a specific cognitive objective: to develop and expand awareness of the various psychotogenic factors triggering the psychotic episodes and, in addition to that, develop strategies to possibly avoid these triggering factors in the future. Important as this may be, one might rightly ask if this is still in line with the psychodynamic approach. Here it might be argued that this procedure is, nonetheless, in the service of integrating the capacity to anticipate and thus avoid the onset of a psychotic episode. In that sense the therapeutic work is not primarily concerned with the integration of the psychotic catastrophe but rather with determining the risk factors for disintegration.

Psychopharmacological drug treatment may contribute to the reintegration of the ego functions. But this does not happen automatically. Although it is true that medication can have a dedynamising effect allowing the ego to reintegrate the world of experience, the issue of the intake of medication as part of the treatment should always be duly accounted for in the course of the therapeutic conversations, in that therapist and patient jointly discuss the question of the use of pharmacological drugs in order to prevent that the patient once again feels disempowered and dispossessed. Medication, to some extent, makes easier the task for the patient to regain his psychic balance and integrative functions, but it can't undertake for the restitution of the ego functions or for the improvement of perceptual and drive regulation experienced as a function of the ego. This will necessarily require the working through of the patient's transference by way of other and additional psychotherapeutic methods.

This working through is so essential, since it may afford the patient a better understanding of him- or herself. And furthermore it is an identity stabilising measure aimed at warding off the (mis)understanding of a self-image of just being 'mad'. What in this approach is and remains of first priority is not to prevent a relapse, but rather to foster and promote the integration of the various levels of psychotic experience into the patient's personality structure.

Chapter 4

Psychotherapeutic work with psychotic patients

The imminent loss of the reality-testing capacity

The loss of the capacity to integrate psychic experiences and the disintegration of personality structure are invariably experienced by the patient as an existence-threatening crisis. The earlier the therapeutic work can start, and the earlier the psychotic dynamic can be understood and thus be integrated, the better the chances for recovery. And that's the reason why it is so vitally important to be able to recognise the pre-psychotic modes of experience and start treatment as soon as possible.

But even if it is not possible to intervene in the disease process or stop the progression of the psychotic episode in the preliminary stages and the patient is already in a more advanced stage when treatment begins, it is always advisable to look back on the pre-psychotic crises. The ability of a psychodynamically informed psycho-education to create a more complex understanding, among other things for the connection between the patient's biographical experiences and his current condition, should not remain unutilised and can often best be promoted by the patient's gaining insight into the dynamics of the pre-psychotic crisis. The therapist whose main concern it is to facilitate the mobilisation of the constructive and healing forces latent within the patient will often have to come to the decision that the best way forward will be to act on different levels and thus carefully contemplate the various treatment options available. In most cases the challenge is finding the right combination of psychodynamic and psychopharmacological treatment.

I am purposely abandoning the term 'prodromal stage' and instead am arguing for using the more favourable term 'pre-psychotic crisis': speaking of 'prodromi' and 'stages' strongly suggest a biologically determined evolution of the disease. If, however, one speaks of a 'pre-psychotic crisis', this leaves open the possibility for alternative pathways of the disease and does, in any case, not implicitly suggest that one is necessarily dealing with a fatal and irreducible biological process. When hearing terms like 'prodromal stage' or 'prodromal symptoms' one is almost forced to the conclusion that what one is dealing with is an organically caused disease.

Viewed from a psychodynamic perspective Günter Lempa (2006) describes, *inter alia*, the following pre-psychotic phenomena:

- There are patients with distinct autistic features or autistic-like behaviour, which can sometimes lead on to 'obsessive and almost addictive-like psychic retreats' (Lempa 2006: 34). The flight into one's own abysmally deep and spectacular imaginary worlds in order to avoid reality's harsh challenges would appear to be one such possibility among others.
- The fear and dread of becoming independent and autonomous can sometimes be immense. This includes that the patient is too frightened to be active and take his life into his own hands and to make own decisions. To the necessity of taking responsibility of his own actions the patient may even react with such a steep increase in panic that he eventually will be caught up in a space where cascades of anxiety affect him to such an extent that he feels falling into an abyss. Conflicts of loyalties towards the parents or other significant others are experienced as so unbearable that it appears even too dangerous to say 'no' to them or else to make a claim for oneself. A particular family dynamic may possibly even fuel such fears and anxieties, for example, if due to unclear roles and responsibilities or vague identities the family structure is constantly changing, but likewise if the family members seal themselves off from the world around them.

Stavros Mentzos emphasises the importance of the psychodynamic understanding of these (and other) prodromal symptoms or forms of psychotic experience and behaviour. Mentzos argues that putting this psychodynamic understanding into practice goes beyond interpreting or diagnosing the symptom, but helps the therapist becoming aware of the productive potentialities contained in any symptom. This psychodynamic perspective will have an immediate impact on the therapist's technique with the advantage that the therapist will presumably not feel too overwhelmed by feelings of powerlessness and hopelessness, but rather encouraged by the awareness of the productive psychotic symptom to tackle the underlying problem and find the appropriate treatment measures.

In order to demonstrate this point Mentzos (2006) refers to a patient, who during the initial interview mentions that he can see that Mentzos has gone mad. This apparent projection was, at this particular instance, obviously the only way to ward off massive psychic pressure and persecutory anxieties and to thus protect the self against the threat of fragmentation. Viewed from this perspective, the projection serves the function of reducing the pressure and tension caused by overwhelming anxieties: 'It is not me, who is mad, but it is him'. This understanding of the symptom may make possible a therapeutic intervention, where not only the patient's fear of becoming mad is addressed and discussed, but also his underlying need for reintegration, which subsequently may lead to the patient's informed consent to the prescription of neuroleptic drugs.

92 Psychotherapeutic work

According to Mentzos the psychotic patient's symptomatology is the attempt at coping with an unbearable dialectic psychic tension, resulting from a basic human dilemma or conflict of, on the one side, the need for the object, that is, the need to establish contact with the object and, on the other side, the protection and preservation of self-identity due to fusion danger through too much proximity to the object. Mentzos refers to the defence function of psychotic symptoms. The dialectical tension resulting from this difficult basic conflict urges the patient to find psychotic 'solutions' – such as, for example, the retreat into an autistic state of mind or the fusional relationship with the object, as described by Lempa – which may not be the best solutions possible, but maybe the only ones that can be realised by the psychotic patient under certain circumstances.

Now, the dilemma or conflict of the patient suffering from an affective psychosis is a somewhat different one: this particular patient has to find a solution to the deficit of self-esteem, which normally manifests as either gross over-valuation of the other or gross over-valuation of the self. For this reason we can conclude that a cognitive approach will not be sufficient as an appropriate preventive treatment measure in the pre-psychotic stage of an affective psychosis. I would argue that it is a psychodynamic approach, from which the patient is much more likely to benefit in order to find an alternative – this time maybe better and more suitable – solution to his basic dilemma.

Thomas Müller (2009) emphasises that in some cases it is very difficult for the clinician to specify precisely the triggering conditions, even though they may hold a highly specific meaning for the individual patient. Nevertheless, Müller argues – and here he proves himself to be a worthy disciple of Stavros Mentzos – that what mobilises the psychotic defence mechanism is always the patient seeing himself confronted with the fundamental conflict of object-neediness and self-safety. If this proximity-distance equilibrium is felt to be seriously menaced, the patient is haunted by persecutory anxieties (due to the object's intrusion or abandonment), which the unstable self cannot contain or compensate for. At the same time an archaic longing for being loved by the object ('object hunger') is evoked. The patient, who feels vulnerable and persecuted, may under certain circumstances have no other alternative than to resort to the psychotic solution: the psychic structure is not only subverted but actively repudiated leading to further fragmentation and thus even augmenting the level of anxiety. An escalation of introjection and projection processes ensues. Omnipotent phantasies predominate. It is important to bear in mind that psychotic mechanisms are ego-accomplishments aiming at omnipotently repairing the self and the object – but finally to no avail.

The compulsion to compensate for what the other is giving – a clinical example

As an illustrative example I am now going to present excerpts of a psychoanalytically oriented psychotherapy of a patient, who had to face several (pre)psychotic crises

Psychotherapeutic work 93

in the course of his therapy. During puberty Mr L. had developed a severe eating disorder. Later he suffered from a personality disorder accompanied by recurrent psychotic episodes.

Mr L. comes from a well-off middle-class family. Because of a serious illness in her childhood Mr L's younger sister requires the mother's whole attention. During the sister's repeated and long hospital stays the mother spends extended periods of time away from home making use of the possibility of the rooming-in system offered by the hospital. During these repeated absences of the mother Mr L. remains under the care of his father who does everything he can to replace the absent mother. The patient is literally mothered by the father. The patient takes after his father, they have the same character, and over time between the two of them a close and intimate relationship develops. The father attaches particular importance to professional achievements although he does not say so explicitly. On top of it, the father harbours excessive expectations in regard to the strict observance of certain values. So, on the one side, there is the parents' overall understanding attitude and, on the other side, their tacit, but all the more subtly intrusive expectations, from which a tricky situation ensues that makes it even more impossible for Mr L. – in all stages of his development – to distance himself from his parents.

Symptom development

What follows is a brief description of the development of the patient's symptomatology with particular emphasis on the pre-psychotic phases. In adolescence Mr L. develops an eating disorder and rapidly emaciates. He finally agrees to undergo psychotherapeutic treatment. When he then, at some point, has to discontinue his treatment with his first therapist I start seeing him. In the course of his treatment he develops pre-psychotic symptoms: there is an 'impressive disinhibition' (cf. Janzarik 1988), a dominance of sensual impressions over the patient's thoughts and thinking, because the affective and sensual impressions intrusively invade consciousness. The patient's delusional beliefs gravely affect and impair his social behaviour (persecutory delusions).

Further symptoms develop as a consequence of the patient's obvious attempts at counteracting decompensation, only leading to further impairments. His overall incapacity to make decisions immobilises him to such an extent that he finally feels incapable of taking any action at all over long periods of time. These symptoms are part of an obsessive-compulsive disorder as it becomes evident only later on in the course of the therapy. This obsessive-compulsive disorder manifests itself in subtle ways and in various everyday life situations: amenable to the laws of magical thinking he is forced to retain a defined sequence with his daily activities, since otherwise the day cannot be brought to a proper end with a good outcome. Although it seems that the eating disorder has been largely overcome the dealing with food needs and eating is still a major problem; he either staves off his nutritional intake; that is, he defers the beginning of his meals, or else the termination of his meal. So the issue of eating still continues to preoccupy his mind for a long time.

To be able to better classify and appreciate justly the different crises the patient had to overcome, I am now going to describe in more detail some significant phases of his therapy:

The leave-taking from his former therapist

His first therapist passed on Mr L. directly to me. The saying farewell to and the final separation from her affects the patient far more profoundly than he initially realises. He was given the possibility to choose his future therapist. So, three months before the end of his previous therapy he comes to see me for a consultation in order to see for himself if he really would like to work with me. He expressly emphasises that he would like to continue therapy with me. But when we actually start working together, it becomes apparent that he finds it very difficult to accept me. Time and again he compares me with his previous therapist. He says that she was much more able to deal with him and to far better understand him.

I accept this devaluation of my person and interpret it as the manifestation of the longing for the absent mother: and in actual fact he had lost his mother to his younger sister early in his life. Due to the loss of his previous female psychotherapist the patient is now faced with the repetition of that earlier traumatic situation with the mother. However, this interpretation makes our working together not easier. There are times, when the patient gets quite agitated and panicky over the feeling that he might have lost something vitally important and irretrievable.

The working through of the emotional hazards

After that there comes a time when Mr L. starts gaining confidence in me. I can sense his despair when he talks about the fears and anxieties he experiences in all sorts of areas of everyday life: he tells me about the emotional hazards of vainly trying to tolerate the proximity to other people, of being incapable of eating in the kitchen when others are around, of being forced to listen to the noises coming from the other rooms in the house. It seems that the boundaries between himself and the others have been lost, and that, despite all his efforts, he is not able to control or re-establish this vital borderline between himself and others – and this is the point in therapy, when the patient in an effort to overcome his resistance is, for the first time, capable to discuss this important issue with me.

Then, the patient decides to start professional training. It is obvious that his own performance demands are so enormous that he is barely able to cope. He obviously wants to do everything well, and he wants to do it even better. As far as the perception of his own competence is concerned, the patient is convinced that he is not at all good at giving lectures, and that he also cannot tolerate being the centre of attention. The emotional strain on him is tremendous, and so he relies upon me as the stabilising and supporting therapist who helps him coming to terms with his emotional hazards in his daily activities.

Friendship

At some point a friendship develops between him and a female friend, which at first goes almost unnoticed: He himself seems most surprised about the fact that he gets along quite well with her nearly from the beginning. But as this relationship is obviously one of the few things that are good in his life he does not bring this issue up in therapy for quite a while. I understand this as a progressive and beneficial behaviour, because it evidences that he can retain something good for himself to which I have no admittance. But on the other hand, it also means that this is an issue – and there have been several others – from which he wants to exclude me, because he evidently does not want to share with me these positive developments. He seems to be afraid of having to separate from me if he admits that in some areas there is actually positive therapeutic development. It is almost as though there is an inner prohibiting agent that is forbidding him to grow up and reach adulthood.

The relationship to the parents

The patient idealises his own parents and the parental home. Mr L. seems to believe that life with his parents was almost like living in paradise. He greatly envies his sister who still lives at home. In his mind the sister is privileged, because she can still enjoy the pleasure to be in close contact with the parents. Only gradually it dawns on him that the parents withheld something vital from him when he grew up: the experience of boundaries. He first becomes aware of it when he realises that the financial arrangements with his parents are totally unclear. He notices that he does not even know how much financial support he is allowed to ask from his parents who generally seem to be willing to give their son everything.

The psychotic crisis

But then he is thrown into a crisis. There is a considerable change in the patient's subjective feeling and this is also the time when his mind begins to deteriorate. He repeatedly complains about the loss of his 'sense of naturalness' he so far took for granted and which creates for him a great amount of sorrow and suffering. He now is much less capable than before to control his ego demarcations, i.e. the ego boundaries between self and others: if he is in the cinema and in the row behind him there is a woman who becomes restless, for example, putting on and off her shoes, this makes him immediately feel extremely troubled. Delusional ideas of having a unique and privileged relationship with some stranger (delusion of reference) may suddenly pop up in his mind, and which he then, by making use of his own reasoning and will-power, has to try to get rid of and out of his mind – and to his great relief he always manages to do so. The train journey which is necessary to attend his therapy sessions puts quite some strain on him. Sitting in the train compartment on his journey it frequently happens that he experiences momentary paranoid delusions (delusions of influence). The lights in the train become so over-whelmingly intrusive that he is overcome by the feeling of being totally blinded by the lights and no longer able to escape them. And, furthermore, there is this humming noise in my consulting room that is hardly audible and coming from my computer, which is at times perceived by the patient like an intensifying tinnitus buzzing ringing in his ears that would not leave his head. He then invariably gets very upset emotionally, since he worries a great deal about his sanity and overall state of mind. His anancastic personality disorder is an aggravating factor in these situations, because it makes him constantly cast doubt on anything and everything including himself.

Together we try to understand what the triggering factors are that invariably lead to these (pre)psychotic experiences. We find out that these are often situations of physical exhaustion, for example, when he does not eat enough, or when he physically overstrains himself and is, at the same time, starved out. But there are other triggering factors that all refer to a concrete situation where the patient has to sustain a transition and where in order to somehow deal with this situation all of his psychic efforts are focused on the immediate present situation: There is plenty of evidence that he has no trouble concentrating, when he is actively involved in working on a clearly defined task, for instance, when he has to produce a written work or to prepare for a test or exam. But if after several hours of writing or reading he has finished this work for his studies and then has no prefixed plan or purpose in his mind what to do next, this is when he enters into such a critical situation that immediately evokes dreaded feelings of loneliness and despair – and that's the moment when the sense impressions become overwhelming and invade consciousness, a situation which then may even lead to paranoid delusions. He manages to re-establish his mental balance no sooner than he has made up his mind on what to do next, in other words, no sooner than he can bring into effect his own intentionality and purposiveness.

Viewed from a wider perspective, it could be said that his mind deteriorates whenever he is confronted with the demand of taking a step forward towards taking responsibility for himself and becoming more independent and autonomous. He finishes his first training and decides to do at once a second one. But this would mean to go through the effort and the strains of moving house and to say farewell to a place and surroundings he has painstakingly become accustomed to, and to venture an important step forward into an unknown future and an unknown sur-rounding in some other place. But there is always this question, which is looming large and which undoubtedly gravely preoccupies his mind: will he succeed to distance himself from his parents and become more independent?

But besides that, there is also the threat of having to separate himself from me, his therapist, he now has been seeing for such a long time. He subsequently considers whether it would be worthwhile to try out to live for some time without any therapy or else to perhaps try out some kind of body therapy. But then again he brings up the issue of working with a female therapist, because he apparently still asks himself, if in his case this might be the much more beneficiary solution. These separation phantasies invariably produce stress and anxiety in him and doubts and uncertainties of how to deal with the future.

At some point we start to discuss the possibility of taking a neuroleptic drug in low dosage. Only after discussing this issue for several weeks, he then is prepared to accept the prescription of the psychiatric medication. My foremost concern as a therapist is that the patient can see the medication not as an agent of disempowering him but rather as providing him with a sense of empowerment and regained stability and particularly of increased competency.

I finally tell him my interpretation of his ambivalent attitude towards me, which I see evidenced by the various symptoms regularly manifesting themselves during the train journey necessary to arrive at his sessions. On the one hand his symptoms can be understood as an impediment – especially if they get worse – preventing him from coming to see me; but on the other hand, these symptoms might also be considered as a good reason to continue his therapy with me and postpone its termination. Viewed in that light, the overwhelming perceptual or sensual impressions are projections of split-off and isolated negative feelings towards me, which then return from the outside to persecute him.

Counter-transference implications in the psychotic crisis

The implications of the patient's struggle for autonomy (i.e. on the one side, his exceedingly strong wish to not develop and psychically grow and, on the other side, his equally strong wish to become independent and autonomous) represent an extremely difficult counter-transference dilemma: To sustain this ambiguity is a particularly challenging and agonising experience for me. If I make any suggestions, what he could do, Mr L. feels undermined and brought under someone else's control and consequently no longer knows anymore what he himself would want to do. If, however, I refrain from giving him any advice, but instead choose to be just the attentive therapist in his presence, he experiences me as if I were his father, who lacks stable contours and thus becomes awkward and menacing and, worst of all, completely inauthentic.

All this makes being understood an essentially ambivalent experience. Understanding leads to the experience of the dissolution of boundaries. But whenever I am taking a more advisory or directive approach, this is experienced by the patient as intrusive and disempowering, as if I wanted to deprive him of his personal rights. What ensues from this is a situation where a simple

98 Psychotherapeutic work

or 'unsuspicious' response is no longer possible, that is, responding to the genuine and real needs of the patient. If, for example, the patient asks me to reschedule or postpone a particular session, this request is not only done on account of the avoidance of overlapping schedules, but also on account of his putting me to the test whether he can or cannot seduce me to give him a maximum of freedom in order to avoid experiencing any feelings of limitation.

After the crisis

The therapeutic efforts of working through the pre-psychotic episodes eventually lead to the patient's regaining a relatively stable psychic equilibrium. Mr L. finally sets aside his sceptical attitude towards the prescription of medication and agrees to take a very low dosage of an anti-psychotic drug. As expected the medication is well tolerated by the patient. Nevertheless, the patient had found it very difficult to reach the point where he could see that the medication might, in effect, be an ameliorative factor in his life. And in that sense the acceptance of medication can also be considered as a clear indication that he is now better able to look after his own needs and care for himself.

What's more, the patient could establish and maintain a trusting and lasting relationship with his girlfriend, which is why they eventually decide to move in together and have a joint home. Mr L. attends therapy on a regular basis. What I find most striking is that from the point on, when the patient had summoned up the courage to criticise me and to voice the issue of the termination of the therapy and thus setting a boundary between him and me, he was no longer haunted by psychotic-like or paranoid delusions during his frequent train journeys on his way to the therapy sessions with me.

While working through this issue the rather complicated relationship to the father increasingly comes into focus. Mr L. tells me about his recurrent dreams, in which the father is watching him from a hiding place in order to see what he is doing and whether he is doing the right thing, etc. It is this over-proximity to the father which he experiences as so burdensome and stressful. He finds it very difficult to talk about these things, because he is afraid that, as a consequence of this, his whole value system might be overturned and that he suddenly might discover that he actually does not come from a good parental home, as he always thought, but rather from a highly problematic one.

After he has completed his first training and then decides to pursue further education, it seems particularly important to Mr L. to address and unequivocally clarify the issue of financial support from his parents. He now feels confident enough to demand from his parents clear rules and a clear arrangement in this area of financial support. Nevertheless, he invests considerable effort in becoming able, at least partially, to finance his studies himself. He considers it a huge step forward that he was capable to find a way out of his former ambivalence and hence unwaveringly pursue one particular professional goal. I now see it as a priority that Mr L. develops a greater understanding and appreciation for his life's path so far, because otherwise there is a danger that Mr L. continues to blame himself for not having become financially independent sooner and still not yet being in a position to support a family etc. It is quite helpful if we both, the patient and I, succeed in the session to reformulate what the patient refers to as deplorable deficits – often accusing himself for them – into desirable goals worth striving for. This eventually enables Mr L. to clearly and unambivalently express his wish to have a family of his own.

A short therapy sequence

At some point in the course of the therapeutic process there is this particular session when Mr L. feels completely misunderstood by me, for which reason he is fiercely accusing me of being totally unable to empathically relate to his desperate situation. The patient obviously refers to the previous session, when at some point I had said to him, certainly not without a certain assertiveness and noticeable affect in my voice, that he, just like other people as well, had to accomplish the task of choosing from among all the existing possibilities and then go ahead and pick one in order to start tackling one real project and thus give up on the other unrealistic projects, which exist only in his imagination. The patient had thought of it as an imposition and an unreasonable and excessive demand. In this context it is worth mentioning that in this previous session it had been rather difficult for me to handle my counter-transference feelings tinged with anger and annoyance in response to the patient's narcissistic demands and his wishful thinking.

In the next session I remind him of our disagreement in the previous session with regard to his not feeling understood by me and his subsequent indignation. While his eyes begin to fill with tears of rage and anger he says to me that it should not be too great a problem for me to comprehend that he had already squandered all the chances and opportunities he once may have had in his life. I then make the attempt to further specify and interpret the point of our disagreement and misunderstanding each other. But there seems to be no chance of getting through to him and Mr L. does not move away from the narrow view that his failing in life is just an undeniable and indisputable reality. I do not waver in my conviction and thus tell him that there is a part in him that resists and refuses to cooperate with his therapist, because this would mean that he actually had to give up on his deceptive flights of fancy of his adolescence including his romantic ideas about his parents. And I also tell him that I think that this is the reason why he refuses to talk about the important fact that he and his girlfriend have moved in together, in other words that he continues to insist that he has not accomplished anything in his life, whereas the fact is that there are obvious indications of recent achievements and developments in several areas of his life. My critically addressing this issue in that particular manner has evidently a reassuring and calming effect on him. And in response to my critical comment he actually comes up with several forward-looking and concrete ideas for the future.

How can this session sequence be interpreted and understood? Each of his attempts at establishing a demarcation line (i.e. boundaries between him and the other) is immediately experienced by Mr L. as a form of destruction, which is apparently the patient's most fundamental conflict or dilemma in life. Any form of separation is experienced as destroying the object. To insist upon his own opinion or his own autonomy is always a precarious venture. Whenever there is a slight move into the direction of increased autonomy or independence, he instantly becomes endangered by the onset of a psychotic crisis and psychotic decompensation, because now his own, previously projected destructiveness returns from without. He experiences himself as hostile, he feels watched and controlled, and the lights forcefully intrude upon him. The split-off and fragmented objects return in the real: the minutely split-off object particles invade consciousness and dominate over the patient's thinking and memory and gravely impair it.

Why is it then that my 'outbreak' (i.e. my slightly too realistic, uncontrolled counter-transference response) has ultimately such a calming and reassuring effect upon the patient, which then gives rise to a more distinct and precise interpretation? There are two significant aspects to be stressed in this context: I proved to be not overwhelmed by the patient's projections into me – admittedly, I was very firm in what I said to him, but I was in no way aggressive or malevolent. In doing so, I set a clear boundary. I showed him where the limits of my patience are, which might be considered as an urgent appeal to Mr L. to finally be prepared to change himself and his general attitude in life. The other equally important aspect is that through my therapeutic action I conveyed to the patient that I am determined to protect our therapeutic work, put differently, that I do not want the psychotic part of Mr L.'s personality getting the upper hand and destroy and nullify the therapeutic progress. By this I have 'staked a claim' and chosen a form of naming, which then may perhaps be integrated into the symbolic world of representations.

Interpretations according to the psychodynamic factor model

Is it perhaps possible to better understand Mr L. and his psychic predicament with the aid of the psychodynamic factor model? The first factor I would like to point out is his hatred of reality: he strictly denies that there are 'facts of life' we all have to recognise and accept. One of these facts is that he can only psychically grow and develop if he accepts the separation from his parents, in other words, if he recognises that they have an intimate relationship from which he is, at least at times, excluded.

He cannot see his own psychic development as something which represents a positive and life-enhancing opportunity. Therefore he has to over and over again undo and ruin it, as it becomes evident in his at times overwhelming ambivalence as a result of which his professional future and career opportunities are severely jeopardised. He can neither accept the passing of time nor the fact that he himself is getting older. And he cannot accept that it is necessary to make decisions for the future, since this inevitably brings with it an awareness of the fact that the vast spectrum of virtually limitless possibilities is already now lost forever (factor: 'recognition of the facts of life').

Then, there is the difficult relationship to his parents, where the boundaries between him and them are blurred, which produces a situation of mutual entanglement from which he only after a great deal of effort and agonising over what to do is eventually capable of finding a way out. It can be said that in his family of origin boundaries are not recognised and respected (factor: 'differentiation of the relationship between self and object'). And so the patient had found a particular solution for himself where all his relationships in his life are built upon a specific economy adhering to the principle of recompense. The parents, but particularly the father, have given the son everything. The patient has, as he himself freely admits, been 'spoiled' by his parents. But this giving has always been tied to a tacit and implicit – and therefore all the more debilitating – condition, namely, that he should give back to his parents, particularly to his father, what he has himself received from them or him, albeit in a primarily immaterial 'currency', in that the son has to shoulder the responsibility for the father's will to live. And indeed Mr L. gives his all for his parents. He lives completely for his parents: by virtue of his own professional success he wants to recompense for the parents' – unfulfilled – wishes and aspirations in their lives. Burdened with this excessive demand he breaks down – but there is also a hidden wish to free himself from this debilitating demand. But because he lacks the capacity to psychically integrate separation or loss he is unable to proceed into the direction of greater independence and autonomy. Any move into this direction has to be instantly reversed, which manifests itself in different ways, first, his eating disorder and, later on, his immobilising ambivalence, which will become even more acute during his recurrent pre-psychotic crises (factor: 'integration of the ego-functions').

Why is it that it is so extremely difficult for Mr L. to distance himself and separate from his parents and lead an independent life? In line with Jacques Lacan's argumentation one could say that in the case of Mr L. separation is a step that has to be repudiated or foreclosed (factor: 'the capacity to represent experiences'). The consideration of the patient's family dynamics provides us with further illuminating insights: in the patient's family of origin there was no encouragement to experience or respect boundaries. A further complicating factor in the patient's case is that not only the boundaries between the self and the object are blurred but also those between the sexes; the beloved father is at the same time the early nurturing and caring mother. This leads to the tacit agreement between the family members: the one who leaves and separates from the others, is harmful and destructive. But of course the issue here is not the actual and real dependency of the father upon his son (i.e. the father who cannot tolerate his son's leaving the parental home), but rather the imago the son has been constructing in his mind on the basis of the father's indirect, vague and tacit communications (factor: 'quality of early object relationships', and in particular: 'recognition and respect of the boundaries of the other').

102 Psychotherapeutic work

The eating disorder that Mr L. has been developing during puberty can be seen as representing in its obvious ambiguity an – of course ultimately failed – attempt at solving the basic conflict of distance and proximity to the object: the patient's striving for autonomy shows in the mad behaviour of not eating, which is, however, also a form of rebellion or provocation, which will ultimately and inevitably turn against himself, not only in terms of his physical health but likewise of his mental health. He severely accuses and denigrates himself for his apparent – feminine – weakness. What makes matters even more complicated is that in doing so he superegoically identifies with the father. The more strict and denigrating the patient is towards himself – just as the father once 'tacitly' imposed his strict demands on him – the less he is now able to detach himself from the father.

It is the psychotic part of the personality of Mr L., which has to defend itself so vehemently against any form of progress or psychic development. I always try to form an alliance with the non-psychotic part of the patient's personality. There is always a sane part of the personality alongside a muddled and unbounded part. Between the two of them a wall of compulsive and magical thinking has to be erected. And since no integration is possible it needs other, more violent psychic strategies to keep the two parts separate from each other which over time becomes an ever more challenging task – and that's why the wall grows steadily higher.

Viewed against the background of Mr L.'s life history, one can understand even better why it is that – whenever he gets along with me quite well in therapy – his past catches up with him and he at once stands under the compulsion to be there for me unconditionally, in other words, to recompense for what I give him. On this condition it is hardly possible to experience himself anymore as an independent and autonomous person and that's the reason why he then has to endure psychotic-like experiences which entail the threat of dissolution of the perceptual and the ego boundaries. And now human contact and closeness are equivalent to giving himself away, or put yet in another way, to once again get enmeshed and entangled in a guilt-laden battle for recompense. It is all but easy for Mr L. to finally admit to himself that this battle is really a battle, and not merely a giving himself unconditionally and devotedly to others – that it is actually a self-imposed radical battle to the point of self-abandonment.

At some point he arrives at one of his sessions and just by the way lets it drop that today he didn't feel like coming to his therapy session. I am so caught off guard that I dig a bit deeper and ask him what he means, whereupon he explains in more detail that he has come to see me for much too long now, without being really able to overcome his crises. Maybe it would be better to do a behavioural therapy with a woman. What he would want to get is real and concrete help, which he does not receive here with me. I understand these statements as positive steps towards a self-determined life rather than a devaluation of our psychoanalytic work. I am glad, after all his agonising efforts to comply with the other, to hear him proffer an independent opinion and making plans for the future which takes him away from the vicious circle of the compulsion to recompense for what the other person, in this case myself, has been giving him.

Psychotic residual conditions as a defence against relationships

Is it possible that psychoanalysis can help the clinician or therapist to discover the life potentialities contained in the patient's negation, even in his most radical 'no'? More precisely: What can psychoanalysis provide to become aware that alongside the object-negating quality of the patient's seemingly negative symptomatology there is also the object-seeking quality of the symptom? In order to elucidate this issue I would like to once again return to Sigmund Freud and in particular to his article on 'Negation' (Freud 1925), where Freud takes up the idea of two positive aspects of negation: The first aspect is that the content of an idea can make its way into consciousness although its emotional meaning remains repressed ('I did not mean to say something insulting', whereas really it was my unconscious intention to do so). The second aspect concerns the question of the differentiation of what is inside and what is outside. What is negated is initially attributed to the outside world. Therefore one can say that negation plays a vital role in differentiating between inside and outside. All that which is not good is perceived as alien and coming from outside: 'You are bad, I am good.'

The post-Freudian contributions of the object-relations theory conceptualise the developmental achievement of becoming able to differentiate between inside and outside as the psychic capacity to make a distinction between self and object. But what are the consequences for the subject if the primary attachment figure does not allow for a development-specific awareness of the boundaries between the self and the object – put differently, if the primary attachment figure does not allow to be established as an object? One possible reason for this could be that there is from the very beginning a lack of affective attunement or resonance because the primary attachment figure ropes in the developing self of the child for her own needs and purposes, so that the developing child is prevented from establishing a vital boundary between 'me' and 'other', and consequently the child is fated to remain a 'cork child' (cf. McDougall 1985: 99) – that is, a part of the mother's self. A particularly desperate form of maintaining distance from the object, described as the work of the negative (*'travail du negatif'*) by André Green, manifests itself in the abolition of perception of (psychic) reality or of one's own feelings and affects with the aim of creating an emptiness acting as a substitution in place of a distance from the object, which has the function of being the necessary condition for the individual's ideational capacity. Prototypical for the work of the negative is the negative hallucination (i.e. the hallucination of an emptiness or void), that is, of a nothingness, which ranges from the abolition of a perception (as in the dreams of the 'Wolf Man') to the extinction of affects and feelings in cases of psychosomatic disorders or in the case of nihilistic delusion (*'delir de négation'*), where everything is emptied out of the mind and the patient is exposed to a void of non-representation and self-annihilations.

This specific understanding of emptiness as a self-created emptiness serving as an attempt at establishing a vital distance from the object – if the intrusion of and

104 Psychotherapeutic work

the separation from the object become so radical and absolute that the necessary conditions of representability in a 'ventilated space' between self and object are not any more given – accounts for the constitutive and positive function of the work of the negative, namely that of being an attempt to create a potential space as described by Winnicott. All of this will have important technical implications for the treatment of psychotic patients. What manifests as a deficiency can no longer be simply described as a failure of the ego functions, or as some kind of a defect, but rather as the patient's – howsoever inadequate, unfavourable and forced – attempt to protect the self through the negation of the affects, of perception of (psychic) reality and of thought.

Being aware of the positive role of the negative dimension in the mind will have an immediate impact on the clinician's therapeutic technique, and gives rise to a number of complex questions that may prove beneficial to the clinician working with psychotic patients:

- Is the phenomenon of self-harming behaviour and self-inflicted injury – which today presents a real and practical challenge to the clinician – to be understood as a loss or lack of self-control? Or perhaps rather as a tacit response to previously suffered traumatising events? Or is it to be viewed as a self-staging of an earlier traumatic event (i.e. a revival of unbearable feelings in the attempt at (re)constituting the self)? The self-inflicted injury conceived of as the repetition of a previously suffered trauma would thus have to be considered as the forced attempt to get rid of a terrible emptiness and nothingness and through self-stimulation bring about some kind of self-experience: If the individual is so utterly overwhelmed and filled with painful emotions, self-inflicted pain would seem to be the last resort to create an otherwise unattainable, perhaps minimal sense of self-efficacy in order to escape – if only briefly – from being merely the passive victim of pain and psychic immobility.
- Is the complete breakdown of communication to the object in case of residual psychotic conditions, in other words, the destruction of the relationship through radical decathexis and total withdrawal from the object to be understood as the attempt at constituting an inner empty space, occupying the place where an inner potential space should have been but never was? – And is under certain circumstances the only possible way to protect the self from repeated violating experiences of intrusion this setting-up of an inner void or vacuum?
- Can the anorexic adolescent girl's letting herself almost starve to death be also understood as a self-sacrificing act to save the parents, who without having to take care of a sick child – or in any case without a child – would be forced to face their own inner void and emptiness, so that the child in a superhuman effort attempts to protect the parents and, as a corollary of this, prefers to remain seriously ill and a child forever and to even risk dying for the parents?
- Can it be said that the suicidal intent, and even the completed suicide, represents also an – albeit desperate – act of communication, for example, if somebody

takes his or her own life, apparently completely unmotivated and in a manner which seems to be utterly alien to him or her; or if the seemingly so far mentally stable individual, who has committed suicide, is then post-mortem declared as having been mentally ill or insane, without the slightest respect or attentiveness for the possible message contained in the act of suicide? The absence (i.e. that which had never found a place in the transitional space of the relationship between self and other) can apparently only now in the radical act of suicide find access to the representation of the absence of representation.

I would argue that we can discover some positive and productive potentialities contained even in the most life-negating symptomatology; and we can find some traces of self-preservation contained even in self-destructiveness. However, I would not like to convey the impression that this presents a plea for 'positive thinking' in the sense of naively 'putting a gloss on things', but rather a passionate plea for 'positivisation' as described by Gaetano Benedetti, who advised all the professionals, clinicians and therapists working with psychotic patients to find and encourage the life potentialities contained even in the seemingly most negative symptoms.

The way of dealing with inner and outer walls – a literary case example

In 1853 Herman Melville wrote a most remarkable story, whose psychological potential has not been fully exhausted up until this day. The story, called *Bartleby, the Scrivener*, can arguably make a significant contribution to the understanding of the 'work of the negative'. It reads like the report on a human being whose entire efforts are focused on the immediate present situation for the sole purpose of setting up and establishing boundaries and a borderline between himself and his surroundings.

The story

The story can be quickly summarised: Bartleby obtains employment as a scrivener in a lawyer's office. Apart from him there are three other scriveners in the office as the reader learns from the memories and impressions of the first-person narrator (i.e. the attorney who directs the office). The attorney and his four employees work in conditions where space is restricted and so Bartleby is allocated a place in the office that allows no view of the outside, since there are walls everywhere that obstruct the view. This squares with the fact that the story is set in New York at the most prestigious address – Wall Street – and in actual fact the reader soon gains the impression of a street of walls: walls are put up everywhere, outdoors and indoors, because even in the office a high folding screen blocks the view.

On the third day Bartleby for the first time emits his most notorious formula of refusal: 'I would prefer not to . . .' Bartleby prefers not to comply with the

106 Psychotherapeutic work

attorney's requests for minor activities and remains in the recess behind the screen. And so he also refuses when the attorney tells him to proofread and collate the two clerks' copies or, a bit later, to reread his own copies. Soon Bartleby is relieved of the obligation to proofread. And it won't be long before Bartleby stops copying altogether, but remains on the premises. Under no circumstances whatsoever he wants to be released. When the attorney asks him to leave Bartleby just does not follow the attorney's request. Bartleby remains standing immobile and upright before a blind wall. The attorney sees himself forced to go to all sorts of extremes to rid himself of Bartleby until he finally sees no other way out but to flee from his own office in order to relocate his law office elsewhere and thus rid himself of Bartleby. But even this drastic step proves to be of no avail: After a while the landlord of the old office in Wall Street calls upon the attorney for help; he informs the attorney that something has to be done about Bartleby who refuses to leave the building. The landlord insists that the attorney must take Bartleby away from there at once. So the attorney sets off for Wall Street and tries to do his best to persuade Bartleby to leave the building, and finally he even tries to take him away with him – but all efforts are in vain. At last Bartleby is taken by the security forces of the local police to prison. Once again the attorney is called upon for help and to speak to Bartleby in prison, because nobody there can figure him out and, on top of it, he now has stopped eating. At his last visit in prison the attorney sees Bartleby strangely huddled at the base of the prison wall lying completely motionless at the ground – that Bartleby soon after that dies is not any more recounted in detail by the first-person narrator. As if it almost goes without saying the reader is just matter-of-factly informed of that incident.

Bartleby time and again utters his 'no', even though he does not act in a consistent manner. With his now famous formula 'I would prefer not to . . .' he refuses to take whatever action he is required to implement. Bartleby himself seems to have no other escape than to withdraw behind his partition every time he utters his formula. He simply refuses to leave the place where he withdraws from anything that might involve getting into contact with others. Finally he has taken up permanent residence in the office rooms, from which he can only be removed through the imposition of enforced measures after all the attorney's hopes of bringing Bartleby back to reason are dashed, because they rest on a logic of presuppositions according to which an employee follows his employer's instructions and demands, and more generally, according to which a person complies with certain explicit and implicit social and relational conventions. His intake of food is gradually decreasing until he stops eating altogether, because he insists on being a man without references, and thus refuses to take anything from others. But the problem solutions of setting up boundaries between himself and his surroundings remain an ever-present concern throughout the story that never stops haunting Bartleby, and which the reader is easily able to relate to through the presentation of concrete and powerful pictures. Bartleby's work place is located near a small window which affords him a minimum of day light coming from outside, but which due to the erection of high walls of nearby buildings affords him no view of the outside world. Not just only outside, but also inside Bartleby's view is obstructed, because the employer has put up a high green folding screen, which prevents direct visual contact but not hearing contact. Bartleby more and more tries to retreat into a cocoon, a womb-like existence. Hardly surprising then that near the end of Bartleby's life in prison (called the 'Tombs') the attorney at his last visit there finds Bartleby lying on the floor curled up in a foetal position: 'Strangely huddled at the base of the wall, his knees drawn up, and lying on his side, his head touching the cold stones, I saw the wasted Bartleby.'

Bartleby is simply planted in the middle of the office without doing anything in particular, and the attorney is incapable of internally distancing himself from Bartleby. At times he idealises Bartleby and is willing to tolerate him and all his peculiarities and oddities; at other times he is determined to throw him out and even kill him – but whatever attempts are made by the attorney he cannot get away from Bartleby. Bartleby does not tolerate any change: 'No: at present I would prefer not to make any change at all.' Bartleby manages to make himself indispensable by distancing himself from his employer through his notorious formula – a paradoxical situation indeed. It is like a shared madness, where the attorney cannot get away from Bartleby, nor can he tolerate being together with him.

The recognition of massive projections and projective identifications

If we as psychotherapists want to make sure to be really of use to patients who inevitably remind us of Bartleby, we should try to assess whether our own attitudes and feelings are influenced by the projected experiences of the patient, in other words, whether our various reactions to the patient are also or perhaps predominantly a response to the patient's attempt to projectively get rid of his or her unbearable feeling states. However, if that is the case the therapist's countertransference experience contains the patient's most urgent messages. It is precisely this aspect which in the story of Bartleby is so masterfully described. And I think, it is most valuable to expand on this in more detail.

First, there is an instant when the attorney idealises Bartleby and enjoys Bartleby's permanent presence. Thus, Bartleby can be said to represent an idealised object which is always present and never absent, and which is projected:

> As days passed on, I became considerably reconciled to Bartleby. His steadiness, his freedom from all dissipation, his incessant industry (except when he chose to throw himself into a standing revery behind his screen), his great stillness, his unalterableness of demeanor under all circumstances, made him a valuable acquisition. One prime thing was this – *he was always there* – first in the morning, continually through the day, and the last at night. I had a singular confidence in his honesty.

> (Melville 1853)

108 Psychotherapeutic work

But then there is another element that has a more adverse effect on the relationship between the attorney and Bartleby, which involves the projection of passive wishes that are – explicitly – experienced as castration wishes:

> Indeed, it was his wonderful mildness chiefly, which not only disarmed me, but unmanned me as it were. For I consider that one, for the time, is a sort of unmanned when he tranquilly permits his hired clerk to dictate to him, and order him away from his own premises.
>
> (Melville 1853)

Later, a depressive mood takes hold of the attorney, in such an extremely strong way he never experienced it before:

> For the first time in my life a feeling of over-powering stinging melancholy seized me. Before, I had never experienced aught but a not unpleasing sadness. The bond of a common humanity now drew me irresistibly to gloom. A fraternal melancholy! For both I and Bartleby were sons of Adam.
>
> (Melville 1853)

But at some point later the attorney's melancholy changes suddenly: he adopts the detached position of the observer, thereby abandoning the empathic attitude:

> My first emotions had been those of pure melancholy and sincerest pity; but just in proportion as the forlornness of Bartleby grew and grew to my imagination, did that same melancholy merge into fear, that pity into repulsion. [. . .] To a sensitive being, pity is not seldom pain. And when at last it is perceived that such pity cannot lead to effectual succor, common sense bids the soul be rid of it. What I saw that morning persuaded me that the scrivener was the victim of innate and incurable disorder. I might give alms to his body; but his body did not pain him; it was his soul that suffered, and his soul I could not reach.
>
> (Melville 1853)

After that, it is a matter only of getting rid of Bartleby. These aggressive impulses and thoughts are idealised by the attorney in a self-celebrating manner:

> As I walked home in a pensive mood, my vanity got the better of my pity. I could not but highly plume myself on my masterly management in getting rid of Bartleby. Masterly I call it, and such it must appear to any dispassionate thinker. The beauty of my procedure seemed to consist in its perfect quietness.
>
> (Melville 1853)

Finally destructive phantasies gain the upper hand: 'Rather would I let him live or die here, and then mason up his remnants in the wall' (ibid.).

Psychotherapeutic work 109

Reconstruction of biographical background

Only at the very end of the story does the reader learn a small detail of Bartleby's biography. The first-person narrator refers – if not to a biographical fact – then at least to a piece of gossip or rumour that came to his ear after Bartleby's death. Rumour has it that Bartleby had previously been a subordinate clerk in the Dead Letter Office at Washington, where undeliverable mail without address is opened, hold in trust for a while before it is then finally burned. Melville's story ends with a strange turn of phrase: 'On errands of life, these letters speed to death. Ah, Bartleby! Ah, humanity!' (Melville 1853). Those letters are messengers of life, which without ever reaching their destination speed to death.

This ending can surely be seen as a metaphor for Bartleby's essential life experience, which in Melville's story carries, however, a principally existential dimension: Bartleby's messages go unheeded and cannot find a recipient. In the Dead Letter Office, in which the undeliverable letters are handled, neither time nor effort is provided for containment. Yet Bartleby reveals a great deal of his innermost thoughts in that he tells of all this to the employer in his mute and silent manner:

- He tells of his self-idealisation, and of his omnipotent phantasy he made up within the narcissistic cocoon he spun around himself.
- He tacitly tells of his unbearable loneliness.
- He discloses his destructive and unacceptably strong aggressive impulses.
- He shows the employer that he himself is totally incapable of mentally digesting or processing or of verbally communicating his earlier experiences of non-attunement. The only way open to him is to project them. Bartleby's speechlessness finds its ultimate expression in the formula: 'I would prefer not to'.

Those who listen very carefully will hear and receive these messages – and in any treatment of psychotic patients the therapist must be attuned specifically to these non-verbal messages. I am going to further elaborate on this issue in the following section.

Therapeutic self-reflection

What would have happened to Bartleby if his direct opposite had not been an attorney but a psychoanalyst? The analyst will presumably not be able to be more attentive to and receptive of Bartleby's non-verbal communications than Melville's attorney who registers within himself all the varying feeling states evoked in him by Bartleby and his peculiar presence. The attorney realises that he feels inclined to rise up against Bartleby and align himself with law and order. But he also becomes aware of opposite phantasies when he wishes to become one in mind and heart with Bartleby. Phantasies of overvaluation and phantasies of devaluation, phantasies of forbearance and phantasies of remorseless rigour alternate in the soul of the employer. One might imagine that the attorney is getting emotionally involved with Bartleby as any devoted psychoanalyst would do with a patient who apparently withdraws from and vehemently resists the idea of any therapeutic alliance. In fact, it seems that the attorney is more than willing to understand and also keen to learn more about the painful life experiences of Bartleby. At the end of the story the attorney even proposes a far-reaching interpretation on the basis of a piece of rumour concerning Bartleby's previous employment in the Dead Letter Office at Washington. So, there is the attorney's motivation to understand Bartleby on the basis of getting to know him better, which is obviously in line with the therapeutic attitude of the psychoanalyst.

But that's about all that Melville's attorney and the psychoanalyst have in common. Just how basic the differences are, will be illuminated by making reference to the following points:

- *Triangulation:* The analyst would have reflected upon the specific interaction and thus would have been able to understand the feelings evoked in him as a counter-transference response, which might have been used to establish an emotional rapport with Bartleby. Through the analyst's self-awareness and self-reflection a new and essential element would have been introduced into the relationship that serves the function of triangulation thus obviating the dyadic impasse the attorney has been drawn into when he, on the one hand, colludes with Bartleby and, on the other, seeks to enforce the norms of law and order against him.
- *Spatial setting:* What framework conditions are required to establish a therapeutic alliance? The analyst would have carefully considered and specified the spatial framework conditions of the therapeutic encounter. Furthermore, the analyst would have tried to understand what impact these specified spatial conditions have upon the relationship and, in particular, what the inner correspondence is between these specific conditions and Bartleby's expectations and fears. The analyst might probably have been concerned about the particular spatial arrangement in the law office with Bartleby situated behind his partition (i.e. the green folding screen), which creates a peculiar and bizarre proximity and simultaneously a distance from his employer.
- *A respectful and accepting attitude:* The analyst would have attempted not to let personal gain or advantage interfere with the Bartleby-encounters. Unlike Melville's attorney the analyst would have not – or at least not primarily – set himself up as a self-staged moral authority in relating with Bartleby, but would instead have registered Bartleby's attacks without judging or condemning them. Despite all refusals the analyst would have made efforts to consistently sustain a positive, respectful and accepting attitude towards Bartleby.

The prolonged duration of the psychotherapeutic treatment as an indication of resistance or the therapeutic avoidance of working with the patient's 'no'

What is it that we can learn from Melville's literary model? First of all, it draws our attention to the fact that residual conditions and apparently negative symptoms as we encounter them in the post-acute stages of a schizophrenic psychosis, but also in a so-called schizophrenia simplex or hebephrenia, are not to be conceived of as an indication of a biologically caused psychosis, but rather to be conceived of as serving an object-seeking function, in other words that these symptoms may have to be understood as the patient's 'no' and as his desperate attempt to get rid of terrible loneliness and to re-establish contact with the object within a – this time finally – more reliable and stable relationship. The acceptance of this would be a first major step towards reaching a better understanding of psychotic suffering. Putting this understanding of the psychotic symptoms and the patient's implicit or explicit 'no' into practice means that we as clinicians and therapists become aware that even the destruction of meaning, the withdrawal from language and speech, and the loss of a meaningful communication may ultimately serve an object-seeking function within – and only within – a viable relationship.

We do have to ask ourselves, however, one difficult and tricky question: Why do we invariably find it so hard to bring the psychotherapeutic treatment of psychotic patients to a close? Is it perhaps because of the fact that the therapist is incapable of altering the psychotic patient's psychic structure, so that the therapist must continue to be there as a stabilising and supportive factor in the patient's life which mainly serves the function of containing unbearable and overwhelming anxieties and imaginations? Or is it rather because of the fact that the therapy, as the treatment goes along, takes on certain aspects from the psychotic experience, such as the denial of the basic facts of life and especially the denial of the passage of time? It is in any case worth considering the possible consequences of both aspects. But there is a third aspect that should at least be briefly addressed in the context of dealing with and tackling the psychotic patient's 'no'.

It is to the credit of Raymond Borens (1993) that in his clinical and theoretical work he focused his reflections on the question why it is that presumably every psychotherapist finds it so difficult to disengage from the relationship with 'his' psychotic patient. Borens comes to the conclusion that what makes it such a difficult endeavour is that in the treatment of psychotic patients the therapist's idealisation of his patient and the specifically intense transference relationship play an important and crucial role. More precisely, through his cathecting the patient the analyst succeeds to create within himself an imaginary space, for which the psychotic patient lacks the inner resources, because he was never given the opportunity to develop within himself a potential imaginary space necessary to make use of and represent his own experiences. But if this idealisation of the patient cannot be resolved and properly worked through in the course of the analytic process, this poses a real problem from which a lifelong dependence of the patient on his therapist may ensue – and in some ways also the other way round.

All this explains the peculiar intensity of the psychotic patient's transference, and also the psychotic patient's total idealisation of and very often abject surrender to his therapist. Yet, only if the therapeutic pair starts dealing with the patient's implicit or explicit 'no', it will be possible for the patient to gain insight into his idealisation of the analyst, which is the necessary precondition to start looking for other ideal objects and to eventually even give up the worshipping and idealising of objects in order to finally bring about a change in the psychotic structure (Borens 1995). In practice, this means that any psychotherapeutic treatment that lasts for a prolonged period of time should be scrutinised to ensure that the continuation of the therapy is not due to the revival of an illusion of timelessness and the illusion of not ever having to separate from the therapist. If we take a look at it from yet another angle, one could say: If psychotic decompensation is the only means possible to avoid separating from the analyst, the psychotic patient will more than likely resort to it. But if this is the case, the patient may already in the course of therapy use the psychotic regression as a lever against psychic development and therapeutic progress.

Psychotic and non-psychotic parts of the personality

Nobody *is* intrinsically psychotic. Even though a person may be overwhelmed with psychotic experience, this does not mean that this person's entire personality is seized by it. Hence, one can say that a person suffers from a psychotic disorder, but there is no justification for stating that a person *is* psychotic. In the light of this linguistic distinction, it is quite apparent that we have to further pursue the question of the relation between the psychotic and the non-psychotic parts of the personality.

In his remarkable and pioneering work on differentiating the psychotic from the non-psychotic parts of the personality (Bion 1957), Wilfred R. Bion introduced an entirely new way of understanding psychosis in that he described in detail the separate functioning of the psychotic and non-psychotic parts of the personality, which had profound and far-reaching implications for clinical practice. Bion argued that the psychotic part of the personality attempts to impose a total withdrawal from reality, but that the ego's contact with reality is never entirely lost due to the existence of a non-psychotic (i.e. neurotic) part of the personality that functions in parallel with the psychotic part, although it is often covered-up or obscured by it, and that is also the reason why the psychotic part can never totally succeed in denying or negating reality. Proceeding from Bion's differentiation Richard Lucas has in recent years developed his own psychoanalytic approach, which is particularly suited for the application within general psychiatry (Lucas 2009). Lucas emphasised that the most common defence mechanisms brought to bear by the psychotic patient are not projections or projective identifications, but rather rationalisations and denial: By making use of these neurotic defence mechanisms the non-psychotic part of the personality is covering up the underlying psychotic modes of experience, so that the clinician runs the risk of succumbing to the patient's rationalisations and consequently failing to notice the underlying psychosis.

In my view, putting the understanding of the differentiation of the psychotic from the non-psychotic part of the personality into practice, seems to be of particular relevance to any clinician, who is working with psychotic patients: When listening to the patient, the clinician or therapist must be aware of the possibility that what sounds like a direct and straight-forward communication from the non-psychotic part of the personality may well be a rationalisation from the psychotic part of the personality which is obscuring and covering up the psychotic parts – but this may have serious clinical implications in that the patient feels not seen, not understood and not valued as an entire person. Now, it is important to point out that apart from the possibility that the psychotic parts of the personality are obscured by the non-psychotic parts, there exists also the reverse possibility, namely that the non-psychotic parts are obscured by the psychotic parts – and this insight is a crucial factor for the choice of therapeutic approach.

The covering up of the psychotic part of the personality through the non-psychotic part of the personality

Let's first start with the more commonly encountered case of the patient, who will do everything in his power to cover up his underlying psychotic experience, because it is perceived as something very ominous and threatening, but also as embarrassing and humiliating, or maybe even because it concerns experiences of physical intimacy the patient is unwilling to share with his therapist or his immediate family. Let me clarify this by an example of a male patient:

> Mr G. lives alone in his own apartment. At a certain point in time he starts feeling increasingly persecuted and watched within his own four walls. When the feelings of persecution intensify, he finally becomes so frightened that he dreads entering the hallway of the building he lives in. Furthermore, he is beset by massive sleep problems, because he is convinced that he must remain awake and watch out for possible intruders who might try to enter his flat and launch a savage attack on him.
>
> Mr G. has been ill for a very long time. He firmly believes that he is a great disappointment for his parents, especially for his father, because he has been unable to take over the father's business, who therefore was all these years totally left to himself with managing the family business. He feels sorry for his parents, since he thinks they should no longer have to work so hard, particularly now that they have reached a more advanced age.
>
> Mr G. more and more loses confidence in himself, and especially loses all his power to tackle anything that has only remotely to do with work or perhaps taking up a job. In the course of time this escalates so far that Mr G. is with

114 Psychotherapeutic work

increasing frequency ending up in total inactivity for hours on end. He says that his loneliness and isolation, and particularly the fact that he has no girlfriend, makes him suffer greatly.

But there is also the non-psychotic part of his personality that allows Mr G. to present himself in therapy as a cooperative and rather adaptive patient. He even manages to learn to become a less compliant person, mainly owing to the group-oriented treatment measures offered to the patients in the clinic. And he even makes a real effort to stand up for his own interests. Eventually Mr G. is becoming a bit more assertive and is even capable of aspiring to play a more active and self-confident role when encountering other people. He also tries to assume more responsibility for his own personal interests.

The psychotic part of the personality remains hidden behind the mask of 'aesthenia'. Due to this weakness and lack of vitality Mr G. is particularly wary of doing or saying anything that could put him in touch with his underlying feelings or affects linked to the psychotic part of the personality. The aim of the psychotherapy is to work on, support and strengthen the functioning of the healthy part of the personality and to further proceed towards the separation of the psychotic from the non-psychotic parts. If, however, the non-psychotic part is not used in the service of working on the psychotic part, but in the service of denying, obscuring and covering up the psychotic part, there is the danger that the underlying psychosis is missed, as a corollary of which – in the patient's subjective experience – the double-entry bookkeeping is perpetuated and probably even intensified. It is therefore essential that we as therapists and clinicians appreciate this fundamental dynamic since failing to notice it may give rise to two major problems:

- It becomes even more difficult to get access to the patient's underlying psychotic thoughts and feelings.
- There is a high risk of psychotic decompensation, if the patient after his premature release from hospital is suddenly faced with a situation, where several triggering stress factors concur. The risk of a relapse has to be considered as being so exceedingly high, because these stress factors had not been addressed within the therapy and thus remained basically unresolved.

If the clinician has to make a decision whether it is safe to release a patient from psychiatric care – especially in case of psychiatric inpatient treatment – caution is always advisable, especially if the therapist or clinician senses the patient's underlying psychotic anxieties. Particularly if the difficult task is in prospect to therapeutically work on his psychotic anxieties, the patient might be liable to deny having any problems. But to succumb to the patient's denial and lack of insight and thus miss the underlying psychotic anxieties and, therefore, agree to the patient's demand to be released from psychiatric inpatient care might be to the detriment of the patient. If, however, the patient and his therapist will jointly face up to the therapeutic challenge of dealing with and remaining sensitive to

Psychotherapeutic work 115

these underlying psychotic experiences and anxieties, the chances are good of successfully averting an otherwise inevitable relapse of the previous psychotic decompensation. No doubt, the work on these psychotic anxieties can be very demanding and stressful for both, patient and therapist, but ultimately those therapeutic efforts that lead to more insight and a deeper understanding of the patient's psychotic predicament will most certainly effectuate a more sustainable recovery with reduced danger of a relapse.

The covering up of the non-psychotic part of the personality through the psychotic part of the personality

One will find that the covering up of the non-psychotic part of the personality through the psychotic part is not very often referred to. The reason for this is not that it is an uncommon psychic strategy, but rather that the clinician often remains unaware of it for a considerable length of time, because it can easily be missed. Clinically it manifests, if the 'mad' part of the personality is employed to avoid the difficult and challenging task of (re)establishing contact with reality. This strategy of covering up the non-psychotic part of the personality is to be conceived of as a flight into psychosis. The following clinical vignette serves as a striking example to elucidate this:

Mr X. has been suffering from chronic schizophrenia for more than thirty years. He is admitted to the clinic – more or less by giving his consent – because he was reported to be in a dangerous state of mind. Some years ago he was diagnosed with a serious heart condition, namely, a progressive degeneration of congestive cardiac failure, which has just been ignored by him. He even keeps on insisting on being fully heart-healthy.

Mr X. leads a very secluded life. He lives most of the time withdrawn from the world, mainly due to the fact that he has not been able to practice his profession as a chemist for nearly three decades. The attempt to establish contact with Mr X. is very taxing for me, his psychotherapist, because he quite obviously is not at all interested in communicating with me. If, as on rare occasions happens, he does talk to me, his words sound exactly like the cliché of a dialogue between a shrink or clinical psychiatrist and a chronically ill psychiatric patient. As soon as I tell him about my observation, he all of a sudden looks straight at me – as I was soon to discover he only is raising his eyes and looking at me, whenever he wants to establish contact with me. In a certain way this makes it a lot easier for me, because I always get to know beforehand, whenever Mr X. is intent and ready, or perhaps capable of establishing contact with me. Incidentally, the patient confirms my assessment by hurling defiance at me, shouting that nothing has changed in the conversations since 25 years – I would like to point out in this context that I actually know Mr X. only since a few days – and that anyhow everything remains always the same and is therefore useless in the face of all the really important and horrendous disasters and tragedies occurring in the world. He then tells me something of his delusions, his apocalyptic phantasies of the end of the world. All of this is documented in detail in the patient's medical file. And so I say to him that all of this is already known to me and that he therefore told me nothing whatsoever new about himself.

After that he once again casts a brief and inquisitive glance at me, whereupon he starts telling me in painstaking detail that he has since long been in a state of progressive decompensation: because of the decompensation of his crystalline lenses he almost can't see anything anymore; and what he can see are just tiny bubbles. He furthermore says that because his entire body is inwrought with these tiny bubbles, there is not even the barest flesh left on his bones, so that anyway he is no longer alive and I should therefore leave him alone and let him drive back into his own world. I then try to find out more about the tiny bubbles. When I ask him, he describes them as CO_2 bubbles.

Since Mr X. is a chemist, he now conveys to me in the guise of his delusion that he clearly is able to recognise that due to his cardiac insufficiency there is too much CO_2 accumulating in his body and that the heart failure he suffers from is life-threatening. But what he does also convey to me is – at least that is how I understand him – that he does not want to live anymore, and that the life he has been leading for so many years now is scarcely worth living anymore. In any case, that is how I interpret his minute description of the decompensation of his body in connection with the tiny bubbles. I let him know what I heard from him and what I made of his words – again he looks at me only to say after a brief pause that he considers it important to keep a clear head and to merely think important thoughts and ideas, not just these everyday nullities and vanities and that therefore he thinks it's best of bringing the conversation to a close at this point. And then, for the first time, he holds out his hand to say good-bye.

The words that I finally received as a gift from Mr X., enabled me to gain a deeper understanding of who Mr X. is. Because I am ready and willing to listen to him and to his words I am eventually rewarded with his cooperation. Initially it was evidently not the patient's intention to communicate to me that he is, at least on some level, aware of his life-threatening heart disease, and that he is simply no longer willing to lead such a monotonous life as in the last few decades, or maybe also that he feels extremely lonely encased in his autistic shell. Only in retrospect and by affectively and positively responding to the patient's delusional ideas, the constitution of a subjectivity was made possible, in other words, a subjective form of self-realisation that as an inner creation was not available to the patient at the beginning of the therapeutic conversation.

This example clearly shows that alongside the psychotic part of the personality there is also the patient's more healthy and depressive striving to deal with the issue of self-worth and the meaning and value of his own life. This raises the question: What was my contribution as a therapist to the patient's moving away from his old strategy to then promptly turn to such relevant, meaningful and life-related issues?

1   First, I would say, I was willing and capable of establishing an emotional rapport with Mr X. And this implies that I did not conceive of his rejecting attitude towards me as a symptom, but rather took it as the patient's personal way of relating to others.
2   And then, I was able to allow my phantasies free rein: Mr X. attributes a role to me, which I never wanted to assume. In his mind I am apparently the director of an obsolescent psychiatric institution, I myself do not want to be, in other words, the replaceable representative of a historically still heavily burdened professional group and still not free from professional blinkers.
3   Furthermore, I attune to the confusing indistinctness and ambiguity inherent in the patient's words, provoked by the patient's negativistic delusion including his belief that everything is in a state of progressive decompensation. And so I have to initially be prepared to bear standing before a blind wall, so to speak; put differently, *not* being able to make sense of the patient's implicit and explicit communications and his psychic condition.
4   During our conversation I try to allow for an ever expanding zone of indiscernibility and indetermination, because I do not want to impose anything upon him and therefore I also refrain from raising the issue of possibly prescribing and taking medication.
5   There are certain things that I say during our conversation that obviously appeal to Mr X. and eventually spark some genuine interest in him, because what I say to him does not oblige him to give anything that he is unable to give. And then, at a certain moment, the patient rewards me for this by offering me the best and most precious that he has to offer: his glance.

Basic to Gaetano Benedetti's concept of positivisation of the mental state of the psychotic patient is his idea of a 'communicative psychopathology', which advises the clinician or therapist to discover, address and encourage the productive and creative potentialities contained in the dynamics of every, even the most severe psychotic symptomatology. Apart from making use of his own countertransferential reaction to the patient, the therapist likewise conceives of the patient's symptom as a form of creatively expressing his own subjectivity, however buried under the patient's overall negativism. And thus it is of crucial importance that the therapist in his effort to empathically identify with the patient, does not only take over the patient's verbal language but attempts to also assess and name the patient's non-verbal implicit language, in order to communicate to the patient that he is the author and creator of all of his experiences and that all of his expressions including his symptoms have a meaning, not only for the other as detached observer, but even more so and in particular for the patient himself. The patient's symptom is thus appreciated as his own interpretation of himself and the world he lives in. Communicative psychopathology viewed in this light can thus be said to conceive of psychopathology as a vehicle of communication and not merely as an index of a destroyed inner world. This gives the patient the possibility to reconstruct himself in a non-psychotic mode of functioning and thus to deal with his depressive-neurotic concerns, at least temporarily.

Pychodynamics of the therapeutic relationship and the use of psychopharmacotropics within the treatment

Psychopharmaceutical medication can sometimes be an indispensable and helpful adjunct to facilitate a promising approach in the treatment of psychotic patients. In general, pharmaceuticals contain biochemical substances, which have a specific effect on the brain metabolism, usually by regulating and channelling the supply of neurochemical transmitter substances, and therefore changing the plasticity of synaptic connections. However, not the biochemical mechanisms of action of the antipsychotic drugs are at issue here, but the psychological effects on all involved in case of medicalisation.

The consumption of medication with antipsychotic substances has generally a direct impact on the patient's psychic structure. The crucial point is that in severe cases of mental illness the use of adjunctive medication may help stabilise the patient's psychic balance to such an extent that the patient, as a result of this, has no longer to be considered as resistant to psychodynamic psychotherapy. One of the reasons for the increased importance and approval of psychopharmacotherapy is its effectiveness in providing symptomatic relief through the dedynamising and dampening effect on the affects and impulses, which often leads also to the patient's regaining a certain equilibrium on the structural level. There are no substantive arguments or assessment criteria justifying that psychopharmacotherapy and psychoanalytic psychotherapy should be mutually exclusive. What I am trying to say here is that in some cases medication may ameliorate the condition for facilitating a psychodynamic psychotherapy, which however is certainly not to say that the use of medication does not affect the therapeutic relationship. How and to what extent this may affect the treatment will be discussed and reflected upon in more detail in the following sections.

The application of medication viewed from the perspective of the therapeutic relationship

What influence does it have on the therapeutic relationship, if it is the therapist who recommends or prescribes psychopharmacotropics during the psychotherapeutic treatment (Abel-Horowitz 1998)? The prescription of medication invariably involves a shift in attitude: The clinician, who is authorised to prescribe medication, is considered an expert or specialist, who has to make a decision and a choice, and who recommends and informs, but who has also set himself the task of surveying the application of medication. What invariably ensues when psychopharmaceuticals have been prescribed is the creation of a new situation, which is imbued with overdetermined transference meanings: from now on the therapist performs the function of a medical consultant and a professional with specialist knowledge; this change in attitude becomes most drastically evident in the treatment of schizophrenic patients. Commonly these patients do not agree to take psychiatric medication, or at least not quite voluntarily. If this is actually the case, there is not only the issue of the therapist in his role of medical expert to be dealt with but, on top of it, there is often also the struggle to cope with conflicts over power.

If the psychotherapist acts simultaneously as a prescriber, who in his function of medical specialist is authorised to offer evaluations and recommendations whether to take medication or not, this inevitably evokes more or less conflictual dynamics in the transference, which may – if worked with and worked through – promote the therapeutic process: The therapist in the transference may become the punishing father, or the protective and caring mother, or perhaps even the absent parent, who asserts a powerful impact on his/her child from afar, or any other imaginable scenario (cf. also Kampfhammer 1997). In the event of such a change in discourse powerful phantasies are almost always evoked. Let's imagine the case of a psychotherapist, who has been working with his patient within a psychoanalytic setting for an extended period of time until the patient eventually becomes more and more depressed, at which point the psychotherapist finally decides to recommend and prescribe an antidepressant medication: What is conveyed to the analysand by way of this recommendation or prescription? Most certainly, it has a considerable impact on the transference and shapes the nature of the therapeutic relationship, which will subsequently be looked at and interpreted in the light of the patient's life history and previous relationship experiences.

When contemplating medication treatment options we have to always be aware of the fact that we are not operating in a sterile field, but rather that there are always forces at work which have to do with biographically pioneered experiences and previous relationships. To promote a negotiated agreement between patient and therapist about the application of medication as an adjunctive measure in the patient's treatment is always a delicate issue and its more or less satisfactory solution will depend on the willingness and capacity to discuss and work through the related transference–counter-transference issues. Take, for instance, the case of an enforced medication, which at a certain point in time became indispensable – if, following this intermittent episode of enforced medication, it is not thoroughly discussed, understood and looked at from the perspective of the psychodynamics of the therapeutic relationship, this certainly will jeopardise and undermine the patient's overall confidence in the therapist and particularly his responsible dealing with prescribing medication.

Medication as a transference object

The medication can assume symbolic meaning as an object of itself and in the therapeutic relationship. We notice that there are always newly emerging self- and object-phantasies to the route of administration of medication: 'In order to be complete I need medication as a crutch, without it I become incomplete and defective.' With this phantasy a female patient, who had obviously accepted the medication as a self-object, which in her mind made her self-concept complete, expressed her firm belief that she will never be able to live by her own efforts and without external assistance. Another patient, who had been diagnosed with schizophrenia, who came to see me for therapeutic support over several years, every once in a while put forward the request to discontinue the neuroleptic medication – which in his case was well-tolerated and caused almost no adverse side effects. It was striking that as soon as I consented to his request, the patient became anxious and extremely restless, although he had not yet stopped taking the neuroleptic drug: the medication apparently had the function of a frame that held him and guaranteed a certain structure and along with it a feeling of homeliness and familiarity, something the patient had been robbed of because of his psychotic breakdown some years ago. Whenever there are any signs of change ahead, the patient is reduced to a state of near panic, because in his mind this signals the beginning of the end. Most therapists are probably familiar with the phobic patient, who is permanently carrying around a tranquiliser in their handbag without ever having to take it – it represents a regulating or transitional object; in other words, it is a memory aid or concretistic item of the therapist and the relationship to him.

In this context of psychopharmacotherapy we need to also take into consideration the psychotherapist's contributions to the psychodynamics of prescribing medication. That the medication can be of maximum benefit to the patient, the therapist has to be prepared to deal with the difficulties created by counter-transference issues and to have the courage to be open to face his own motives and influences in applying psychopharmacotherapy (Rubin 2001). And so there is not only the patient's but also the therapist's transference with regard to the medication to be dealt with. For instance, the therapist may recommend the use of medication because he wants to ward off his own insecurities and anxieties related to the patient's symptomatology. But it can also be the case that the therapist's resistance or reluctance to prescribe medication is on account of the medication becoming a symbol of the unwanted, merely tolerated third, which is experienced by the therapist as an interference or even as a threat to the patient-therapist relationship as well as the therapist's own psychotherapeutic ego-ideal.

The exploration of counter-transference issues will often bring to light useful information of the therapist and patient having different agendas (Purcell 2008). Already the indication to start using the medication may be influenced by the clinician's counter-transferential attitude: the prescription may be a precipitate reaction to the patient's cry for help; or else it may be an attempt at getting rid of the patient or, put differently, to medicate away the patient's symptoms – if we, for instance, just realise how Janus-faced an expression like 'tranquilise a person' is! Harmless though it may sound superficially, our primary association to it on a deeper level is: enforcement and foreign control.

Medication and newfound self-assertion and self-efficacy

The patient, who has been thrown into a severe crisis, frequently can benefit from the medication no sooner than the issue of the patient's need for a sense of autonomy and self-control has been recognised and jointly discussed by therapist and patient. It will, of course, make a huge difference, whether the patient feels the medication was forced upon him and thus robbed him of his last bit of authority and self-control, or whether the patient has the feeling that the medication has bestowed him with a sense of empowerment, has provided him with the experience of newfound self-assertion and the ability to act, in short, has restored his sense of self-efficacy. This also explains why in the case of the manic patient the dedynamising and dampening effect of the psychopharmacological drug is commonly experienced as a loss of autonomy of action and why these patients might refuse taking medication. By contrast, the schizophrenic patients, who are suffering from hallucinations and persecutory anxieties, will usually feel relatively comfortable and even grateful for the opportunity to take medication and experience it as improving the quality of their lives.

But the medication will prove effective in terms of the patient's positive experience of newfound self-assertion and self-efficacy only then, if the prescribing process is integrated into the framework of the psychodynamic reflection on the therapeutic relationship and the patient's unique character and personality. Viewed from the opposite side, the issue can also be phrased as: If the psychopharmaceutical medication has a beneficial effect on the psychotic experience, which subsequently brings about a relaxation in the therapeutic relationship, this may allow the patient to be more open to psychotherapeutic interventions. So, there may be fruitful and positive interactions, or there may be detrimental and negative interactions between the therapeutic work on the psychodynamics of the therapeutic relationship and the patient's experience of enhanced self-efficacy as a result of taking medication.

It thus becomes evident that the application of psychopharmacotropic medication is only *one* factor in the treatment of psychotic patients. Socio- and psychotherapeutic support are equally important factors. There are many indications that medication proves most effective, when psychopharmacotherapy is combined with psychodynamic psychotherapy.

Chapter 5

Psychotherapeutic engagement with psychotic patients

Concluding remarks

Relating to psychotic patients or persons in psychotic states makes us aware that they never actually cease to see themselves confronted with the challenging task of solving difficult dilemmas that are related to basic human conflicts every human being has to come to terms with in his or her own life. From this ensues the need to recognise that the psychiatric psychotherapeutic treatment approach is inevitably also caught up in a variety of (partly ethical) dilemmas. In any case, there seems no benefit gained from adopting a too rigid position when dealing as psychotherapists with psychosis. What I mean to say is that we have to shift our focus and introduce flexibility into our thinking:

1   The therapist has to tune into the patient's psychotic mode of experiencing and thus, at least temporarily, live the patient's catastrophes almost as if they were his own. At the same time, the therapist must always keep sight of the fact that the other person may suddenly appear in all his or her alienness or otherness, something which has to be recognised and accepted in all its peculiar qualities inherent in human beings. A psychodynamic approach makes it possible as well as necessary to get emotionally deeply involved with the psychotic patient. In order to overcome his distant attitude and develop a more empathic attitude towards the psychotic patient, the therapist needs to absorb the patient into himself, in other words, identify himself with the patient while at the same time acknowledge his otherness.

2   Therapeutic commitment to the psychotic patient does not benefit from focussing too keenly and eagerly on an attitude of attempting to achieve a cure ('*furor sanandi*') rather than aiming to further the psychotic individual's potential; but nor does it benefit from an attitude that considers and accepts the psychotic patient's othernesss and alienness as an unalterable fact, since this may make the therapist feel increasingly uncomfortable and desperate and ultimately overcome by feelings of the therapeutic enterprise being a hopeless struggle against an unchangeable condition or defect. The history of psychiatry is replete with examples showing what terrible consequences may follow out of the incapacity to tolerate the dilemmatic tension situated

Concluding remarks 123

between the opposite poles of the desire to achieve a cure (change) and the acceptance of the psychiatric patient's alienness (otherness).

3   Any psychotherapist working psychodynamically with patients in psychotic states must – however strong his own personal commitment may be – not lose sight of the important fact that he is not – and must not be – the only supportive factor in the patient's life, in other words, the therapist must keep in mind that his role is not confined to providing individual psychotherapy for his patient and that providing support on a broader, possibly communal scale for the psychotic patient to come to terms with his condition may be an equally essential requirement. That psychopharmaceutical medication plays almost in any case a crucial role to ease the pathway in relating to the psychotic patient is not the result of a failure or surrender of psychodynamic psychotherapy, but rather a necessary coming-to-grips with the fact that psychosis is a complex and multidimensional human phenomenon. It is crucial, in my view, to always bear in mind that individual psychotherapy is only one of many other factors in the treatment of psychotic patients which is, however, the main and sole focus of the current book. But perhaps we now can see more fully why it is that no single human being becomes psychotic by him- or herself, and even more so, why no single psychotic individual will get better on his or her own (or even *à deux*). Any psychodynamic therapy working with psychotic patients has to also pursue the tasks and accountabilities of social psychiatry, which involves to recognise the patient's need for a containing environment and effective community care; but which involves also to provide support for family members and close relatives. Yet, the opposite also applies: Any social psychiatry that finds the unexamined human life worth living and thus does not find it necessary to endeavour to take account of psychodynamic understanding is at risk of dwindling into mere social management.

4   Every psychotherapist who decides to get involved with psychodynamically oriented work with psychotic patients can draw upon valuable concepts and models of the mind applicable to psychosis – to make this clear to the reader has been one of the prime concerns of the current book. The personal encounter with psychotic patients is always a huge challenge, which urges us to bring to bear our own professional experienced-based knowledge and particularly to retain our own critical faculties when listening to the psychotic individual. But no matter how experienced we may be in the field of psychiatry or psychotherapy, we always need to be very wary at any overvalued ideas of being able to just apply and bring to bear our professional knowledge, because ultimately nothing can prepare us for what awaits us when personally encountering and emotionally getting involved with a person in an acute psychotic state of mind. To be sure, competent treatment of psychoses requires specialised professional knowledge and relies upon a number of preconditions as described in detail in the factor model in one of the previous parts of this book. The point I am trying to bring across here is: A strong personal commitment alone is not sufficient, because without a solid and profound

124 Concluding remarks

training and recurrent further education for those professionals involved in the area of psychosis the demands will not only be much too high, but it would have to be considered as careless or even negligent treatment of patients. Yet, theoretical knowledge alone is equally insufficient, because without personal commitment no effective treatment results will be achieved.

The psychiatric-psychotherapeutic treatment of psychotic disorders does normally not take place in a 'purely' psychotherapeutic setting that has beforehand been discussed, negotiated and then finally mutually agreed upon by patient and therapist together. If it is understood and accepted that the adherence to a chosen setting serves a crucial function in the therapeutic process, then a great deal has been achieved already. So we can see that the need to understand the psychodynamics of psychoses is not only, and perhaps not even primarily of relevance for the psychiatrists or therapists psychotherapeutically treating psychotic patients, but equally and perhaps even more so for the various professionals working in general psychiatry who very often have to deal with irritatingly difficult and disturbing situations. And thus I would want to argue that it is important that not only the practising psychoanalysts are familiar with the psychodynamic perspective of psychoses, but also the different professionals working in the acute care unit of a psychiatric hospital, or the social workers in the field of rehabilitation and prevention, or the specialists in the field of pharmacology.

And now finally, I just want to add one more thing: If this book serves the purpose of being of some help to practising clinicians or professionals, and, furthermore, serves the purpose of encouraging readers to contemplate and perhaps to increase their readiness to further examine the important issue of psychosis, a good part of its intended goal will have been achieved.

References

Abel-Horowitz, J. (1998). Psychopharmacotherapy During an Analysis. *Psychoanalytic Inquiry* 18: 673–701.

Ambrosini, A., Stanghellini, G. and Langer, A. (2011). Typus Melancholicus from Tellenbach Up to the Present Day: A Review about the Premorbid Personality Vulnerable to Melancholia. *Actas Españolas de Psiquiatria* 39(5): 302–311.

APA. (2013). *Diagnostic and Statistical Manual of Mental Disorders*, fifth edition (DSM-5). Washington, DC: American Psychiatric Association.

Arnim, A. von, Joraschky, P. and Lausberg, H. (2007). Körperbilddiagnostik [Diagnostics of Body Image]. In P. Geißler and G. Heisterkamp (eds), *Psychoanalyse der Lebensbewegungen* [*Psychoanalysis of Life Movements*]. New York: Springer, pp. 165–196.

Benedetti, G. (1983). *Psychosentherapie: Psychoanalytische und Existentielle Grundlagen* [*The Therapy for Psychosis: Psychoanalytic and Existential Foundations*]. Stuttgart: Klett.

Benedetti, G. (2002). *Der Geisteskranke als Mitmensch* [*The Mentally Ill Person as Fellow Human Being*]. Göttingen: Vandenhoeck & Ruprecht.

Bick, E. (1987). The Experience of Skin in Early Object Relations. In M. H. Williams (ed.), *The Collected Papers of Martha Harris and Esther Bick*. Perthshire: Clunie Press, pp. 114–118.

Bion, W. R. (1957). Differentiation of the Psychotic from the Non-Psychotic Personalities. In W. R. Bion, *Second Thoughts*. London: Karnac, pp. 43–64 [1967].

Bion, W. R. (1959). Attacks on Linking. In W. R. Bion, *Second Thoughts*. London: Karnac, pp. 93–109 [1967].

Bion, W. R. (1962). *Learning from Experience*. London: Karnac [1984].

Blankenburg, W. (1971). *Der Verlust der natürlichen Selbstverständlichkeit* [*The Loss of Natural Self-evidence*]. Stuttgart: Enke.

Bleuler, E. (1911). *Dementia praecox oder Gruppe der Schizophrenien*. Leipzig: Deuticke [English-language edition: trans. J. Zinkin, *Dementia Praecox or the Group of Schizophrenias*, New York: New York International Universities Press, 1950].

Borens, R. (1993). Fragmentarische Überlegungen zur Psychose [A Glimpse into Psychosis]. *RISS* 22: 40–48.

Borens, R. (1995). Das fehlende Nein: Ein Beitrag zum Verständnis der Psychose [A Lack of 'No': Contribution to an Understanding of Psychosis]. In G. Lempa and E. Troje (eds), *Psychoanalytische Technik, ihre Anwendung und Veränderung in der Psychosentherapie*: *Forum der psychoanalytischen Psychosentherapie* 10: 50–65.

Britton, R. (1998). *Belief and Imagination*. London: Routledge.

126 References

Broome, M., Bottlender, R., Rösler, M. and Stieglitz, R. (eds). (2017). *The AMDP System: Manual for Assessment and Documentation of Psychopathology in Psychiatry,* 9th edition. Göttingen: Hogrefe Publishing.

Burgoyne, B. and Sullivan, M. (1997). *The Klein–Lacan Dialogues.* London: Rebus Press.

Ciompi, L. (1982). *Affektlogik [Affect and Logic].* Stuttgart: Klett-Cotta.

Conrad, K. (1958). *Die beginnende Schizophrenie [Incipient Schizophrenia].* Stuttgart: Thieme [1979].

Eissler, K. R. (1971). *Talent and Genius: The Fictitious Case of Tausk contra Freud.* New York: Quadrangle Books.

Elkisch, P. (1959). On Infantile Precursors of the 'Influencing Machine' (Tausk). *Psychoanalytic Study of the Child* 14: 219–235.

Foucault, M. (1973). *Birth of the Clinic.* New York: Vintage.

Foucault, M. (1984). *Madness and Civilization: History of Insanity in the Age of Reason.* London: Tavistock).

Frank, M. (1986). *Die Unhintergehbarkeit von Individualität [The Ineluctability of Individuality].* Frankfurt a.M.: Suhrkamp.

Freud, S. (1911). Psychoanalytic Notes on an Autobiographical Account of a Case of Paranoia (Dementia Paranoides). In J. Strachey (ed.), *The Standard Edition of the Complete Psychological Works of Sigmund Freud,* vol. XII, pp. 9–82.

Freud, S. (1914). On Narcissism: An Introduction. In J. Strachey (ed.), *The Standard Edition of the Complete Psychological Works of Sigmund Freud,* vol. XIV, pp. 73–102.

Freud, S. (1915). The Unconscious. In J. Strachey (ed.), *The Standard Edition of the Complete Psychological Works of Sigmund Freud,* vol. XIV, pp. 166–215.

Freud, S. (1923). The Ego and the Id. In J. Strachey (ed.), *The Standard Edition of the Complete Psychological Works of Sigmund Freud,* vol. XIX. pp. 12–66.

Freud, S. (1924). The Loss of Reality in Neurosis and Psychosis. In J. Strachey (ed.), *The Standard Edition of the Complete Psychological Works of Sigmund Freud,* vol. XIX, pp. 183–187.

Freud, S. (1925). Negation. In J. Strachey (ed.), *The Standard Edition of the Complete Psychological Works of Sigmund Freud,* vol. XIX, pp. 235–239.

Freud, S. (1927). Fetishism. In J. Strachey (ed.), *The Standard Edition of the Complete Psychological Works of Sigmund Freud,* vol. XXI pp. 152–157.

Gadamer, H. G. (1960). *Truth and Method.* New York: Continuum [2004].

Glatzel, J. (1978). *Allgemeine Psychopathologie [General Psychopathology].* Stuttgart: Enke.

Gonther, U. and Schlimme, J. (2011) (eds). *Hölderlin und die Psychiatrie [Hölderlin and Psychiatry].* Bonn: Psychiatrie Verlag.

Green, A. (1983). *Life Narcissism, Death Narcissism.* London: Free Association Books.

Green, A. (1986). *The Work of the Negative.* London: Free Association Books.

Green, A. (1997). *On Private Madness.* London: Karnac.

Gruhle, H. W. (1953). *Verstehen und Einfühlen [Understanding and Empathy]: Gesammelte Schriften.* Heidelberg: Springer.

Hartwich, P. and Gruber, M. (2003). *Psychosen-Psychotherapie [The Psychotherapy of Psychosis].* Stuttgart: Steinkopff.

Haug, H. J. (2002). Psychopathologie mit Glossar [Psychopathology by Glossary]. In F. Müller-Spahn and W. Gaebel (eds), *Diagnostik und Therapie psychischer Störungen.* Stuttgart: Kohlhammer, pp. 738–752.

References 127

Heim, R. (2005). Paarungen, Passagen – Das Imaginäre zwischen M. Klein und J. Lacan [Pairing, Passages – The Imaginary in Klein and Lacan]. *Journal für Psychoanalyse* 44: 35–60.

Holzhey-Kunz, A. (2002). *Das Subjekt in der Kur: Über die Bedingungen psychoanalytischer Psychotherapie* [*The Subject on the Couch: On the Preconditions of Psychoanalytic Psychotherapy*]. Vienna: Passagen.

Holzhey-Kunz, A. and Läpple, A. (2008). *Existenzanalyse und Daseinsanalyse* [*Existential Analysis*]. Paderborn: UTB.

Janzarik, W. (1988). *Strukturdynamische Grundlagen der Psychiatrie* [*Structural Dynamics: A Foundation of Psychiatry*]. Stuttgart: Enke.

Jaspers, K. (1913). *General Psychopathology*. Baltimore, MD: Johns Hopkins University Press [1997].

Kapfhammer, H. P. (1997). Psychotherapeutische und pharmakotherapeutische Ansätze in der Behandlung von depressiven Störungen [On the Psychotherapy and Pharmacotherapy in the Treatment of Depressive Disorders]. In P. Buchheim (eds), *Psychotherapie und Psychopharmakologie*. Stuttgart: Schattauer, pp. 31–54.

Klein, M. (1946). Notes on Some Schizoid Mechanisms. In M. Klein, *Envy and Gratitude and Other Works*. London: Virago Press.

Küchenhoff, J. (1998). *Teilstationäre Psychotherapie* [*Psychotherapy in the Day Hospital*]. Stuttgart: Schattauer.

Küchenhoff, J. (2003). Psychotherapie und die Anerkennung des Fremden: Kommentar zu D. Orlinsky [Psychotherapy and the Acknowledgement of the Alien: A Commentary of D. Orlinsky]. *Psychotherapeut* 48: 410–419.

Küchenhoff, J. (2005). *Die Achtung vor dem Anderen* [*Respecting the Other*]. Wissenschaft Weilerswist: Velbrück.

Küchenhoff, J. (2006a). Braucht die internationale klassifizierende Diagnostik noch die Psychodynamik – und wozu? [Is the International Classification in Psychiatry in Need of Psychodynamics – and Why?] In H. Böker (ed.), *Psychoanalyse und Psychiatrie*. Heidelberg: Springer, pp. 205–222.

Küchenhoff, J. (2006b). Denken an den Anderen [Thinking of the Other]. *Psychoanalyse im Widerspruch* 35: 7–25.

Küchenhoff, J. and Warsitz, P. (1993). Zur Theorie der psychoanalytischen Psychosentherapie, oder: Gibt es eine Umkehr der Verwerfung des 'Namens des Vaters'? [On the Theory of the Psychoanalytic Treatment of Psychoses]. In R. Heinz, D. Kamper and U. Sonnemann (eds), *Wahnwelten im Zusammenstoß: Die Psychose als Spiegel der Zeit*. Berlin: Oldenbourg, pp. 163–180.

Küchenhoff, J. and Warsitz, P. (2017). *Labyrinthe des Ohres: Vom therapeutischen Sinn des Zuhörens bei psychotischen und anderen Erfahrungen* [*Labyrinth of the Ear: The Therapeutic Relevance of Listening in Psychotic and Other States*]. Würzburg: Königshausen & Neumann.

Lacan, J. (1988). *The Ego in Freud's Theory and in the Technique of Psychoanalysis: The Seminar of Jacques Lacan, Book II, 1954–1955*. Cambridge: Cambridge University Press.

Lacan, J. (1993). *The Psychoses: The Seminar of Jacques Lacan, Book III, 1955–1956*. London: Routledge.

Lacan, J. (2006). The Function and Field of Speech and Language in Psychoanalysis. In J. Lacan, *Ecrits: The First Complete Edition in English*. New York: W. W. Norton & Company, pp. 197–268.

128 References

Lempa, G. (2006). Schizophrenie-Screening und anschließende Frühintervention [Screening for Schizophrenia and Early Interventions]. In G. Juckel, G. Lempa and E. Troje (eds), *Psychodynamische Therapie von Patienten im schizophrenen Prodromalzustand*. Göttingen: Vandenhoeck & Ruprecht, pp. 21–41.

Lucas, R. (2009). *The Psychotic Wavelength: New Library of Psychoanalysis*. London: Routledge.

McDougall, J. (1985). *Theaters of the Mind: Illusion and Truth on the Psychoanalytic Stage*. New York: Basic Books.

Meltzer, D. (1975). Adhesive Identification. *Contemporary Psychoanalysis* 11: 289–310.

Melville, H. (1853). *Bartleby, the Scrivener: A Story of Wall Street*. Project Gutenberg. Retrieved from www.gutenberg.org/ebooks/11231.

Mentzos, S. (2006). Psychodynamische Diagnostik und Therapie psychotischer prodromaler Syndrome [Psychodynamic Diagnosis and Therapy in Psychotic Prodromal States]. In G. Juckel, G. Lempa and E. Troje (eds), *Psychodynamische Therapie von Patienten im schizophrenen Prodromalzustand*. Göttingen: Vandenhoeck & Ruprecht, pp. 42–53.

Mentzos, S. (2009). *Lehrbuch der Psychodynamik. Die Funktion der Dysfunktionalität psychischer Störungen* [*Textbook of Psychodynamics: The Function of Dysfunctionality in Psychic Disorders*]. Göttingen: Vandenhoeck & Ruprecht.

Mishara, A. (2011). Klaus Conrad (1905–1961): Delusional Mood, Psychosis, and Beginning Schizophrenia. *Schizophrenia Bulletin* 36(1): 9–13.

Money-Kyrle, R. (1981). *The Collected Papers of Roger Money-Kyrle* (ed. D. Meltzer). Perthshire: Clunie Press.

Müller, T. (2009). Die psychotische Transformation der Persönlichkeit [On the Psychotic Transformation of the Personality]. *Psyche* 63: 748–772.

Müller-Spahn, F. and Gaebel, W. (eds) (2002). *Diagnostik und Therapie psychischer Störungen* [*Diagnostics and Therapy of Psychiatric Disorders*]. Stuttgart: Kohlhammer.

Ogden, T. (1992). *The Primitive Edge of Experience*. London: Karnac.

Ogden, T. (1994). The Analytic Third: Working with Intersubjective Clinical Facts. *International Journal of Psychoanalysis* 75: 3–19.

OPD Task Force (ed.) (2009). *Operationalized Psychodynamic Diagnosis OPD-2. Manual of Diagnosis and Treatment Planning*. Bern: Huber.

Orlinsky, D. (2003). Störungsspezifische, personenspezifische und kulturspezifische Psychotherapie: Erkenntnisse aus Psychotherapieforschung und Sozialwissenschaften [Specifity of Disorders, Personality and Culture: Results of Psychotherapy Research and Social Sciences]. *Psychotherapeut* 48: 403–409.

Pankow, G. (1975). *Gesprengte Fesseln der Psychose* [*The Shackles of Psychosis – Burst Open*]. Munich: Kindler.

Peirce, C. S. (1983). *Phänomen und Logik der Zeichen* [translation of *Syllabus of Certain Topics of Logic*]. Frankfurt a. M.: Suhrkamp.

Purcell, S. (2008). The Analyst's Attitude Toward Pharmacotherapy. *Journal of the American Psychoanalytic Association* 56: 913–934.

Racamier, P.-C. (1982). *Die Schizophrenen* [*The Schizophrenics*]. Heidelberg: Springer.

Roazen, P. (1973). *Brother Animal: The Story of Freud and Tausk*. Harmondsworth: Penguin Books.

Rosenfeld, H. (1964). *Psychotic States: A Psychoanalytical Approach*. London: Karnac [1990].

References 129

Rosenfeld, H. (1987). *Impasse and Interpretation: Therapeutic and Anti-therapeutic Factors in the Psychoanalytic Treatment of Psychotic, Borderline and Neurotic Patients.* London: Routledge.

Rubin, J. (2001). Countertransference Factors in the Psychology of Psychopharmacology. *Journal of the American Academy of Psychoanalysis* 29: 565–573.

Sacerdoti, G. (1990). Paul-Claude Racamier. Antoedipe et ses destins. *Rivista Psicoanal.* 36: 742–760.

Saussure, F. de (1916). *Course in General Linguistics.* Glasgow: Fontana [1977].

Scharfetter, C. (2002). *Allgemeine Psychopathologie [General Psychopathology].* Stuttgart: Thieme [English-language edition: *General Psychopathology*, Cambridge: Cambridge University Press, 1980].

Schneider, G. (1995). *Affirmation und Anderssein: Eine dialektische Konzeption personaler Identität [Affirmation and Otherness: A Dialectical Model of Personal Identity].* Opladen: Westdeutscher.

Schneider, K. (1980). *Klinische Psychopathologie [Clinical Psychopathology].* Stuttgart: Thieme [English-language edition: *Clinical Psychopathology*, New York: Grune & Stratton, 1959].

Schreber, D. P. (2000). *Memoirs of my Nervous Illness.* New York: New York Review Books.

Segal, H. (1957). Notes on Symbol Formation. *International Journal of Psychoanalysis* 1957(6): 391–397.

Sennett, R. (1998). *The Corrosion of Character: The Personal Consequences of Work in the New Capitalism.* New York: Norton.

Steiner, J. (1993). *Psychic Retreats.* London: Routledge.

Tausk, V. (1914a). On the Origin of the 'Influencing Machine' in Schizophrenia. In P. Roazen (ed.), *Sexuality, War and Schizophrenia: Collected Psychoanalytic Papers.* New Brunswick, NJ: Transaction Publishers, pp. 185–219.

Tausk, V. (1914b). On the Psychology of the Alcoholic Occupation Delirium. In P. Roazen (ed.), *Sexuality, War and Schizophrenia: Collected Psychoanalytic Papers.* New Brunswick, NJ: Transaction Publishers, pp. 95–118.

Tellenbach, H. (1961). *Melancholie [Melancholia].* Heidelberg: Springer [English-language edition: *Melancholy*, Pittsburgh, PA: Duquesne University Press, 1980].

Thomä, D. (2002). Der bewegliche Mensch: Moderne Identität aus philosophischer Sicht [The Flexible Person: Modern Identity from a Philosophical View]. *Forum der Psychoanalyse* 18: 201–223.

Tustin, F. (1972). *Autism and Childhood Psychosis.* London: Hogarth Press.

Vogt, T. (2007). Verliebt – verkannt – verrückt [In Love – Misunderstood – Mad]. In P. Widmer (eds), *Psychosen: Herausforderung für die Psychoanalyse.* Bielefeld: Transcript, pp. 183–204.

Volkan, V. (1995). *The Infantile Psychotic Self and its Fates: Understanding and Treating Schizophrenics and Other Difficult Patients.* New York: Jason Aronson.

Waldenfels, B. (1990). *Der Stachel des Fremden [The Sting of the Alien].* Frankfurt a. M.: Suhrkamp.

Waldenfels, B. (1997). *Topographie des Fremden [Topography of the Alien].* Frankfurt a. M.: Suhrkamp.

Weizsäcker, V. von. (1950). *Diesseits und jenseits der Medizin [Within and Beyond Medicine].* Stuttgart: Koehler.

WHO. (2016). *International Statistical Classification of Diseases and Related Health Problems*, 10th revision (ICD-10). Geneva: World Health Organization. Online version. Retrieved from http://apps.who.int/classifications/icd10/browse/2016/en.

Winnicott, D. W. (1971). *Playing and Reality*. London: Tavistock Publications.

Wyss, D. (1973). *Beziehung und Gestalt* [*Relationship and Gestalt*]. *Entwurf einer anthropologischen Psychologie und Psychopathologie*. Göttingen: Vandenhoeck & Ruprecht.

Index

acute psychotic disorders 7–8
adhesive identification 46
affect-logic 12
affect-regulation 79
affective psychosis 92
alien, recognition of 16–20, 122–3
alpha function 49
AMDP 4
analytic third 68
Andreas-Salomé, L. 36
anthropology 10
Antoedipus 61–3, 72
attacks on linking 80
autism 44–7
autistic-contiguous position 44–5, 47

Bartleby, the Scrivener 105–12
Benedetti, G. 65–8, 86, 105, 117
Bick, E. 45
Binswanger, L. 10
biogenesis 35–7
Bion, W. R. 43–4, 47–50, 52–4, 58, 80, 112
biopsychosocial perspective 36–7
bizarre object 48
Blankenburg, W. xii, 13
Bleuler, E. 44
body 37–40, 75–7, 88
Borens, R. 111
Boss, M. 10
boundaries *see Bartleby, the Scrivener*; object relations
Britton, R. 61

Ciompi, L. 12
classifications *see* psychiatric classifications

clinical example (Mr L.) 92–3, 96–7; counter-transference 97–8; factor model 100–2; former therapist 94; friendship 95; parental relationship 95; post-crisis 98–9; psychotic crisis 95–6; symptom development 93–4; therapy sequence 99–100; working through of the emotional hazards 94–5
communicative psychopathology 67–8, 117–18
concrete thinking 31–3
Conrad, K. 11–12, 35
contact barrier 49
containing-function 49, 82, 88–9
counter-transference 56–7, 97–100, 107, 119–20
covering up (personality) 112–13; of the non-psychotic part 115–18; of the psychotic part 113–15
creativity 67–8
culture 16

Daseinanalysis 10–11
dead objects 80
delusion 21; disorders 6–7; as projection 21–6; reality 33–5; as weltenaufgang 26–7
deobjectalising function 74
depressive disorders 8
depressive position 42–3
descriptive diagnostics *see* psychiatric classifications
destructiveness 58–60, 68, 74–5
development 47–50
diagnosis ix–x
diagnostic classification *see* psychiatric classifications

132 Index

dialectic thinking 19–20 *see also* interpersonality
difference 54–8
differentiation *see* object relations
dilemma 64
disorder 2–3, 67
drive integration 74–5
drugs *see* medication
DSM 5 1

ego-functions 78–9, 101
Eissler, K. R. 36
Elkisch, P. 38
emptiness 103–4
ending 111–12
experience, learning from 48–9
experiential spaces 60–1, 67, 80

factor model 70–1; clinical example interpretations 100–2; multidimensional understanding 83–6; objectifiable psychic capacities 78–80; psychotherapist's basic attitude 86–7; quality of object relations 80–3; relational dynamics 87–9; subjective experience 71–7
facts of life, recognition of 71–2, 88, 100–1
fetishism 50
foreclosure 50, 79–80, 101
Foucault, M. xi, 14
Frank, M. 15
Freud, S. 21, 36, 58, 75; delusion as projection 21–6; delusion as weltenaufgang 26–7; language 29–31; narcissism 27–9; negation 103; reality 33–5

Gadamer, H.-G. 3
Gestalt psychology 11–12
Glatzel, J. xii–13, 73
Green, A. 59–60, 73–4, 80, 103
Gruhle, H. 6

Heidegger, M. 11
Hölderlin, F. ix–x
Holzhey-Kunz, A. 11

ICD-10 5–8
identity 15, 64, 66
impressive disinhibition 78
incommensurability 14–15
individuality 14–15

Influencing Machine 37–40
inpatient treatment 88–9, 114
integration of drives 74–5
interpersonality xii–xiii, 15–20, 67–8

Janzarik, W. 12, 78
Jaspers, K. 4, 9

Kernberg, O. F. 15
Klein, M. 29, 40–4, 52–3

Lacan, J. 50–3, 58, 79, 101
language 24, 29–31, 79–80, 85–6; concrete thinking 31–3; difference 54–8; symbolic order 50–3
learning from experience 48–9
Lempa, G. 91
libido theory 28–9
Lucas, R. 112–13

medication 89, 118, 123; self-assertion/ self-efficacy 121; therapeutic relationship 118–19; as transference object 119–20
Meltzer, D. 46
Melville, H. 105–12
mental apparatus 78–9
Mentzos, S. 63–5, 73, 91–2
metaphor 32
minute splitting 47–8
Money-Kyrle, R. 62, 68
Müller, T. 92
multidimensional understanding 83–6

narcissism 27–9, 59–63
negation 103–5
neurosis 1–2

object relations 27–9, 40–4, 53, 59–60; differentiation 72–4, 101, 103–5; quality of 80–3, 101
objectifiable psychic capacities 78–80
objectification 14
Ogden, T. H. 44
On the Origin of the "Influencing Machine" in Schizophrenia 37–40
operationalisation 4
Operationalised Psychodynamic Diagnostics (OPD) 78
organising capacities 78–9
Orlinsky, D. 9
otherness *see* recognition of the alien

Index

Pankow, G. 88
paranoid-schizoid position 40–2, 47
Peirce, C. S. 32
person 14–15
personality 14, 112–13; covering up the
  non-psychotic part 115–18; covering up
  the psychotic part 113–15
pharmacological drugs *see* medication
phenomenology 11–12
physical disease 8
positivisation 65–8, 86, 105, 117
power x
preconditions 47–8
pre-psychotic crisis 90–1
projection 21–6, 107–8
prolonged treatment time 111–12
psychiatric classifications 1–5; ICD-10 5–8
psychiatric hospitals x–xi
psychogenesis 35–7
psychopathology 9–10, 13–14; affect-logic
  12; anthropology 10; Daseinanalysis
  10–11; phenomenology and Gestalt
  psychology 11–12; structural dynamic
  12
psychopharmacotropics *see* medication
psychotherapist's basic attitude 86–7, 110
psychotic disorders (ICD-10) 5–8

quality of object relations 80–3

Racamier, P.-C. 61–2, 72
rationalisations *see* covering up
reality relation 33–5
reality-testing 90–2
recognition of the alien 16–20, 122–3
recognition of facts of life 71–2, 88,
  100–1
recovery 26–7
reference person 82
relational dynamics 87–9
relativisation 61
reparation 43, 92
representation 60–1, 79–82, 101
reputation x
residual condition 103
retreat 60
reverie 81
Roazen, P. 36
Rosenfeld, H. 58–9

Sacerdoti, G. 62
Saussure, F. de 32
Schneider, G. 17
Schneider, K. 14
Schreber, D. P. 21–4
scientific house 69–70
second skin 45–6
Segal, H. 31–3
self-image *see* body
separation 82
separation-intrusion dilemma 73
setting *see* spatial setting
sexuality 24–6, 75
social psychiatry 123
solutions 92, 122
spatial setting 110, 124
speech *see* language
splitting, minute 47–8
Steiner, J. 60
structural dynamic 12
subjective experience 71–7
subjectivity 14–15, 66–7, 86–7
symbolic equation 31–3
symbolic order 50–2, 82
symbolisation 31–3
symptoms xii, 63–5, 86–7, 91–2

Tausk, V. 29, 36–40
Tellenbach, H. 10
theory-free presupposition 3–5
therapeutic relationship 86–7, 110, 118–19
time 72
transference 28, 58, 87, 89, 111–12,
  119–20
transitional spaces 60–1, 67, 80–1
triangulation 61–3, 87–8, 110
Tustin, F. 46

value 65
Vogt, T. 50
vulnerability–stress–coping model 36–7

Waldenfels, B. 18–19
ward 88–9
Weizsäcker, V. von. 14
weltenaufgang 26–7
Winnicott, D. W. 44, 60, 73
working-through *see* transference
Wyss, D. 15